CENSORSHIP:
FOR & AGAINST

CENSORSHIP:
FOR
&
AGAINST

INTRODUCTION BY HAROLD H. HART

Hart Publishing Company, Inc.

New York City

Contents

Introduction

Back in 387 B.C., Plato, one of the world's greatest philosophers, suggested that Homer's *Odyssey* be expurgated for immature readers. Around 250 B.C., a Chinese monarch consigned to the flames every single book or writing that contained any of the teachings of Confucius.

In 1244, the *Talmud,* a book revered by the devout, and pored over by generations of Jewish scholars, was burnt on charges of blasphemy and immorality. Roughly 400 years later, Martin Luther's translation of the *Bible* suffered the same fate in Germany by papal fiat.

The list is endless. It includes the works of Dante, Boccaccio, Erasmus, Michelangelo, Cervantes, Galileo, Shakespeare, Sir Francis Bacon, Descartes, Milton, La Fontaine, Moliere, Locke, Swift, Swedenborg, Voltaire, Fielding, Rousseau, Kant, Jefferson, and even the poet, Percy Bysshe Shelley. The roster of great writers who have been banned at one time or another constitutes a literary Who's Who. In our own era, the catalog of the interdicted includes Anatole France, de Maupassant, George Moore, George Bernard Shaw, Oscar Wilde, Sir Arthur Conan Doyle, Havelock Ellis, Henrik Ibsen, Maurice Maeterlinck, Arthur Schnitzler, Gabriele D'Annunzio, Rudyard Kipling, Theodore Dreiser, Bertrand Russell, Jack London, Upton Sinclair, James Joyce, Sinclair Lewis, Eugene O'Neill, Aldous Huxley, William Faulkner, Walt Disney, John Steinbeck, Erskine Caldwell, James Farrell, Ernest Hemingway . . . is there any need to go further? There is hardly a great writer who has not been offensive to some people in authority.

Within recent months, President Nixon denounced the findings of a commission appointed by President Johnson to investigate ways and means of controlling pornography, obscenity, and writings deemed to adversely affect the morals of the American community. Before the findings of the commission were actually published, it was revealed that this body had drafted a report which was in direct contravention to what its sponsors believed such a commission would urge. Consternation resulted. Some people sincerely proclaimed that if the report of the commission were heeded, it would mark the moral demise of the American republic. Other people pointed with equal vehemence to the long list of literary martyrs whose works, during the ages, had been reviled, only to find fairly complete acceptance when moral indignation sufficiently subsided to permit an appreciation of the basic literary merit of these writings.

To most minds, an enormous chasm separates trash pornography from the literary products of serious writers who do not scruple to faithfully report life as they see it in all of its manifestations, including intimate details of sex. These two kinds of writing are accounted as poles apart. Yet any machinery set up to regulate literature would apply the same kind of review, the same kind of surveillance, and the same kind of arbitrary judgment to both kinds of writing. The difference is that censorship hinges on subjective opinion. What is prurient and offensive to one person is merely titillating to another; what is titillating to the second person is but mildly entertaining and inconsequential to a third.

This book is addressed to those who would like to unravel the tangled threads of our laws and our mores. Does the open presence of salacious magazines on our newsstands lead to depravity? Do the photographs of what were hitherto considered private parts corrupt the young? Since four-letter words have become part and parcel of cinema dialogue, has the moral fiber of the community been weakened? In what manner have peep-shows and blue movies affected the welfare of society?

The partisan answers to these questions, stated from every philosophical, sociological, and psychological viewpoint, constitute the material of this provocative book.

HAROLD H. HART

CENSORSHIP:
FOR
&
AGAINST

Presently film critic and contributing editor for SATURDAY REVIEW, *Hollis Alpert was formerly a contributing editor for* WOMAN'S DAY *and editor for* THE NEW YORKER. *Mr. Alpert is the recipient of one of the annual Film Directors Guild awards for "Distinguished Contributions to Film Criticism."*

Mr. Alpert's articles and short stories have also appeared in ESQUIRE, PLAYBOY, MC CALL'S, PARTISAN REVIEW, NEW YORK TIMES MAGAZINE, HARPER'S, *and other publications.*

He has written four novels: THE SUMMER LOVERS, SOME OTHER TIME, FOR IMMEDIATE RELEASE, *and* THE CLAIMANT; *and has published a biography,* THE BARRYMORES, *and a book on film,* THE DREAMS AND THE DREAMERS. *Mr. Alpert is presently working on a new novel and on another book on film*

Hollis Alpert

THE IDEA OF CENSORSHIP, particularly when it is aimed against pornography, has its attractions. What could be seemingly more wholesome than newsstands cleansed of those obnoxious little weekly sheets filled with gleeful celebrations of sexual acts, the more perverse the more gleeful? In what way would the community—any community—be harmed if stores purveying stacks of photographs, glossy magazines, and film strips devoted to illustrating what used to be known as private parts were closed down by police order? Or if cinema houses featuring acts of "love," natural and unnatural, were shuttered? Little would be lost, really.

Even so, I am against censorship.

Over the years, I have had occasion, for journalistic reasons, to examine the question of censorship. I have met and talked to censors; I have been called as an "expert" witness in court cases aimed at suppressing certain films. I have viewed a good part of the Kinsey Institute's collection of pornographic film material and talked to members of the staff. I have read a great many of the available works, legal, sociologic, and psychiatric, on the subject. Nothing I have encountered has changed the opinion stated above.

This is not to say that I, personally, have not been offended by some of what I have encountered. Pornography, according to the dictionary on my desk, is "writings, pictures, etc., intended to arouse sexual desire." It is nonsense to claim, as some do, that there is no such thing as pornography, and that the use of the word indicates something suspicious about the mental and emotional state of the accuser. (There *can* be something suspicious, of course.) Pornography, simply, does intend to arouse sexual desire, and it fails as pornography if it doesn't. The problem is, for the habitual fancier of the stuff, that it takes more and more to arouse; and as a result, the tendency is for pornography to go farther and farther beyond the pale. Unfortunately, there are limits; and eventually, pornography, even for the addict, becomes dull and stale. The problem for the non-addict is that it becomes increasingly offensive.

What I dislike most about pornography is not the fact of its existence, but the level of its taste which, for the most part, is abysmal. Pornography represents a market—literary, journalistic, and cinematic—for unimaginative clods, neurotics of many different persuasions, and the untalented everywhere. All such professional matters such as style, taste, craft, and artistry give way to the tasteless, the brainless, the mercenary, the scatological, the obscene. What is so annoying about obscenity, however it may be defined, is the mockery of human aspirations it essentially represents. I do not admire those who so proudly flaunt the banner of their sexual liberalism, for they mock what has meaning for me.

Therefore, I am not for pornography; I am merely against censoring it.

I do not regard pornography as an evil, but some of

it I do regard as an abomination of sorts. I do not know if exposure to pornography harms either the young, the middle-aged, or the old, but this is not to say that it does not have its effects. It obviously increases the incidence (to use a Kinsey Institute term) of masturbation; but since we hear that masturbation is not harmful and that it is difficult to masturbate to excess, this would not seem to be necessarily a harmful effect.

I don't share the zeal of those who claim for pornography certain benefits for the repressed, the frustrated, the bewildered, and the confused; but I can see where, in certain cases, it might help overcome inhibitions, unwanted modesty, lack of ardor. Yet talking or a modicum of alcoholic drinking can achieve pretty much the same results. As an antidote for boredom and loneliness, pornography may well have some positive value. And by its very frankness, pornography may actually represent an improvement, educationally speaking, for the young who pick up their sexual knowledge on the street or even in some of those earnest sex education courses in schools.

But, again, its therapeutic value needs establishing far more than has been done up to now. In no country where the question has been studied has it yet been found that pornography increases crime. Where rape has been found to be on the rise, it is almost invariably due to social and economic conditions, not to the presence of pornography. While it probably does lead to more sexuality—conjugal and private—for those exposed and attracted to it, pornography does not seem to lead to much in the way of sexual abuse, and here I am speaking primarily of violent forms of sexuality.

In prisons, however, where pornography clearly is not present, sexual abuse, particularly of the homosexual kind, has become a matter of shocking public knowledge.

So I see very little reason to forbid pornography, except that I don't happen to like it.

On the other hand, the mentality of those censors I have met, and of those who advocate censorship, has often filled me with foreboding. All too frequently they have a way of equating pornography with "Godless un-American Communists," and the like. They cite religious tracts, even the Bible (generally overlooking *The Song of Solomon*) as "scientific" reason for their opposition to pornography and for the straitjackets they would impose on publishing and film making. The zeal with which they have attempted to counterattack against the glut of smut is worrisome in itself, revealing, perhaps, of a secret attraction to what they publicly proclaim as "sinful." Beware he of the impassioned rhetoric. All too often his voice, his words, his tone, remind of the righteous Goebbels.

But it is hardly news that there exists a tremendous amount of cant and hypocrisy among those who assume that a battle against pornography is a battle for law and order. While researching material for *History of Sex in Cinema,* a lengthy series published by *Playboy Magazine,* I found that the very pillars of our society—veterans' groups, patriotic organizations, policemen and firemen—were the principal supporters of that hoary American institution, the "stag party." During these evenings one or two hours of a collection of stag reels would be shown to an all-male audience, and where did the evening's entertainment come from? Often enough from the local police or fire chief—confiscated, of course.

While testifying for the release of *I Am Curious—Yellow* and other cinematic works confiscated by U. S. Customs, I was interested to find that in conversation afterward with U. S. Attorneys, a good many of them were not at all in agreement, personally, with the views they presented to the jurors. "Of course the film should be shown," said one young assistant district attorney, "it's really all a kind of infighting." Those twelve good men and true didn't exactly convince me either that the jury system was the best way to achieve a fair verdict.

In one case the attorneys for Customs didn't even bother to make a case for their point of view. They merely exhibited the film in question to the jurors, most of whom seldom left their television sets at night. They had no way of knowing precisely what was commonly shown in theaters across the country and around the world. The attorneys counted on only one thing: that they would be shocked by what they saw. They were, and they declared the film guilty. Of what? Of offensiveness to them, naturally.

And just as naturally, an appeals court overturned their verdict.

But of judges, too, I happen to be suspicious. One U.S. District judge, while upholding a Customs seizure of a film, presumably saw more of a sexually nefarious nature in it than I did; and the horrified language he used to describe those "unspeakable acts" was remarkably similar to what I once heard thundered from a pulpit. Too little separation of church and state, in other words.

Thus, I am inclined to think that pornography and what to do about it should be taken out of the legal sphere entirely. Lawyers and judges use terms like "indecent" without bothering to define "decency." Is killing a stranger in a strange land "decent?" Our decent soldiers do it every day, are encouraged to do it, and are not termed indecent except when they rape one or more of the local women. "Does the film appeal to the prurient interest . . .?" I have long given up attempting to discover what "prurient interest" means—not even the dictionary is of much help here. "The average member of the community." Who is he? And where is this community? Times Square? Scarsdale? Spanish Harlem? Birmingham, Alabama?

The legal battle continues to be fought over a terrain that is inadequately defined, and perhaps cannot be. It may not even exist any longer.

For look what we have: pornography shown in hundreds of theaters, openly; magazines of a crudity unimaginable just a few years ago; "revolutionary" newspapers filled with erotic junk.

In 1964, when my colleague (Arthur Knight) and I began to look into the erotic content of films, beginning with a clip of Fatima, who electrified Chicago's Columbian Exposition in 1893 with her "dance of the veils" and was subsequently immortalized on film in 1906, the stag film was very much underground, photographs showing male and female organs were still taboo, and movies were still obeying a set of restraints known as the Production Code. All that has changed in a mere half-dozen years.

Fatima, we discovered, was first victim of movie censorship. Peep show patrons had been vouchsafed a glimpse of her belly as she undulated, and the authorities of that day quickly stenciled picket fences over the offending portion of her anatomy. It was not more than ten years before the question of movie censorship reached the august halls of Congress; we very nearly had a national censorship statute. And the agitation for such a statute has not died down to this day.

What agitated censors in 1906, 1916, 1926, and 1936, would strike us as silly and laughable today. A bit of revealed nudity, for instance, as in *Ecstasy,* brought out the Comstockery in thousands across the land. Remember how long it took for one of the literary masterpieces of our century, *Ulysses,* to be sold publicly? It was not hard to reach a conclusion that standards of morality have varied, not to say gyrated, from period to period. Yesterday's obscenity is not necessarily today's. Would that all pornography were as gracefully written as, say, *Fanny Hill.*

But one thing has always existed and presumably always will: the urge to create pornography. And even more widespread is the curiosity it evokes and has evoked in untold millions. All efforts to suppress pornography have failed. If made illegal, it springs up illegally. If made legal, it springs up legally. Presumably, we will always have it. And in a measure never envisioned at a time when Victorian gentlemen took up their pens to relate their erotic experiences, real or imagined.

For technology has made pornography the realm of everyman. When it was discovered that the home movie camera could be employed to record bedroom activities in private, processing plants, in self-protection, refused to develope such intimate and illegal (then) goings-on. But there was always that unscrupulous employee who knew how to turn a buck by channeling furtive prints into the furtive stag market. Thus, in the Kinsey Institute collection and many private ones, are 8 mm and 16 mm films made by amateurs and employing amateurs who were mortified to discover (when, on occasion, the police knocked on their doors) that their private activities were being viewed by thousands.

Surcease came in the form of the Polaroid camera. Stills could be taken and developed instantly without recourse to a lab, and one wonders how much effect this "development" had on the stock of the corporation. More realism came with the Polaroid color camera. One reason, perhaps, that Americans were so ready for public pornography was that they had become so adept at producing it privately.

Then came the home video outfit, an expensive toy, surely, but its uses at home immediately evident for those with the insatiable urge to view the sexual behavior of themselves and sometimes intimate friends and sometimes intimate strangers.

Now, upon us, is the cassette and cartridge recorder, much cheaper, much simpler. Just as television brought havoc to the film industry, the home visual recording devices may wreck the public pornography industry. Instantly erasable, a record need never be there for prying officials.

That is why I strongly suspect that the legal terrain has all but vanished. Within another few years, there may be only one way of quelling the production of pornography and the voyeuristic habits it entails. And that is to bring on "Big Brother," which would amount to electronic surveillance and eavesdropping in every suspected home, in corn fields and on boats, in barns, garages, and garrets.

And that is the main reason I am so strongly opposed to the censorship of pornography, for it would require, sooner or later, a vast national (even international) effort, and *1984* would be here long before its time.

Must we live with it then?

Probably so. But should an actual community wish to control its availability, it does have a certain amount of legal leeway. The Supreme Court has already ruled that a community, a legally defined entity such as a township or a county, can "protect" its young by prosecuting those who purvey it to those under a certain age.

If sexual debasement has been ruled out of court, so to speak, as it has been by many, many "sexologists," psychiatrists, and so-called experts on the subject, surely the debasement of taste has not. And there are ways to make clear to the community why pornography usually represents a nadir level of taste. This judgement can be made on the theater owner who prefers to show "X" films over the less gamier kind because "it sells better." No reason not to let him know, through editorials and in community meetings, that his profit motive does not necessarily make him an admirable member of the community.

But censor him not, please, for the dangers in such action are too great.

The current flood of pornography may well be a symptom, but not with any certainty, of a moral decline. What *has* declined is the hold of religious faith, doctrine, and institutions over human impulses and desires. Even among the more devout, a demarcation now is being made between sexual and spiritual morality. With an increasing degree of scientific inquiry into the nature of human sexuality, sex has been taken out of the realm of the morally harmful and has been given literally a clean bill of health when practiced, so the legal language tells us, among consenting adults. Pre-adult sex is on the rise, too, according to gynecologists. For proof they simply cite the prescriptions for pills and other contraceptive methods dispensed to girls fourteen and fifteen years old. "The change," said one veteran woman gynecologist, "has been particularly striking during the past five years."

One aspect of the generational gap is the difference between how young people and their elders view the sex act. Among the older generation, there is still evidence of guilt and anxiety over sexual behavior that varies from what they assume to be the norm—and that norm being the sexual act practiced primarily for the purpose of procreation between females over eighteen and males over twenty one. Taboos, though seldom spoken, still exist. The newer generation has tossed aside most of these taboos. Many among them practice experimental and communal forms of co-habitation. Sex is taken for granted, is thought of as natural, healthy, and an expression of a loving nature. Not by all young people, certainly, but by larger percentages than in previous generations. Community standards—by which censorship has traditionally justified itself—vary widely and extremely and often within the same community. No code of censorship could possibly do justice to the liberalized attitudes toward sex that exist today.

The day may not be far off when the commonly accepted standards of today may totally reverse themselves. In fact, right now the most commonly approved sexual activity—marital copulation aimed at producing an offspring—is being viewed with alarm by many. For the population explosion, long due, is now imminent. The population projections for ten, twenty, and thirty years from now are eerily frightening. Already, in several states abortion has been legalized. But the awful pity of it is that the most economically and educationally blighted groups reproduce the most and perpetuate the problems that create the most stress in this society and others. A new sexual ethic—already existing in many groupings— that substitutes pleasure and release of tensions as its primary goals certainly makes more practical sense if the human race is to survive with any degree of comfort. For there would now seem to be a real need to channel sexual instincts so that they do not result in a cancerous surplus of population.

Perhaps today's pornography can even be regarded as a primitive expression of society's as yet inchoate recognition that sex, divorced from its procreative aspect and even from romantic and sentimental notions of love, can have its positive values. And it can also be regarded as evidence of the widespread frustration that exists in the sexual area, for pornography gets its appeal from its fantasy portrayal of sex. Fantasies arise when instincts are frustrated. In pornography females of any age and racial or ethnic coloration are ever-willing. Males are ever-potent. Thus, whether in the printed word, in photographs, or moving film images, pornography presents to the reader and the viewer fantasy situations that have something to tell us about the human sexual condition.

The artist, viewing his fellows through his personal vision, has through the ages attempted to portray what he sees and to present his understanding of it. Censorship in his case has perpetrated heavy and sometimes reprehensible blunders. Such recognized literary artists as Joyce and Lawrence were for many years relegated to pirated editions that were sold from beneath the counter. What untold artistic riches still reside, barred from the gaze of civilized man, in the Vatican's rumored collection of erotic treasures? The censor, when presented with this kind of evidence of artistic repression, usually has as his answer that a few geniuses may be deprived of their potential publics, but the many will benefit. But how? The censor, by hoping to bar all that he deems reprehensible, commits errors of taste at least equal to those committed by the most foul of pornographers. For each rules out a vast spectrum of gradations and distinctions.

Of the two dangers, restrictive censorship on the one hand and unrestrained pornography on the other, the latter would seem to be the lesser, by far. For the former can create real harm. The unscrupulous politician can take advantage of the emotional, hysterical, and neurotic attitudes toward pornography to incite the multitude towards approval of repressive measures that go far beyond the control of the printed word and the photographed image. Even with a report from a presidential commission that concluded that no societal or individual harm had resulted from the existence of pornography, highly placed officials still took the warpath against its dissemination. Since there seems to be no substantive base for the officials' stand, one must suspect other motives, the simplest one being, perhaps, that of corralling the votes of conservative elements of the population. Implicitly asking for censorship, they overlook the question of who should do the censoring. Whom shall we trust? Whom can we trust? How shall we agree on standards and criteria? Perhaps they don't really care.

I rather suspect that, left alone, the various media tend to regulate themselves. The largest mass medium, television, presents no pornography at all that I know of, unless it be that of violence which some would translate into fantasy sexual sadism and masochism. Thus disguised, much pornography finds its way into the most respectable channels.

Movies are regulated by their markets, and major film companies now espouse four main grades of entertainment which tend to take into account existing types of theatrical exhibition and audiences.

Radio has only the disguised kind of pornography—actually, no more than mild erotic stimulation—that comes from certain kinds of music and suggestive lyrics.

Magazines run a vast gamut; but no one is prevented from reading *Commentary* or *Harper's* by the fact that girlie publications are sold at the same corner newsstand.

Actually, the human mind is so various in its interests that its concentration on pornography takes but a minute portion of its attention. It is at worst a flea that bites an elephant. It requires little effort to overlook it entirely. It does take enormous effort to try to do something about it; and in the long run, it is no more productive than flailing at windmills.

Msgr. Joseph Howard is Executive Secretary of the National Office for Decent Literature, a position he has held since 1963.

He received his M.A. and S.T.L. from St. Mary of the Lake Seminary in Chicago, and was granted a Licentiate in Canon Law from the Gregorian University in Rome.

Joseph Howard

A FRIEND IS LECTURING about pornography in a Chicago suburb when a listener rises and says: "I am not in favor of dirty literature any more than you, but neither am I concerned about it. My wife and I know what our daughter reads. We encourage her to read *good* books. Isn't this the answer?"

My friend is adjusting his Adam's apple and groping for some brilliant reply when a voice comes in loud and clear from the back of the room.

"Sure, it's the answer. Unless, of course, she gets raped by a guy who doesn't have a father like you, and who's been climbin' the walls after reading a closet-full of nudie magazines, like the case of John So-and-so's daughter a couple weeks ago."

The guy in the back of the room, without realizing how profound he really is, keynotes this whole business of salacious litter-ature. Pornography, like prejudice and poverty, is catching. Its deadly germs infect alike Sister Superior and Henry Miller, Ralph Ginzberg and the little old lady who just stepped up to the Blessed Virgin's altar to light a candle, the minister's son, and the convict's daughter.

The night the Speck decision was rendered (Richard Speck, slayer of eight Chicago nurses, was convicted by a jury and sentenced to death), a Chicago talk-telephone radio show was discussing capital punishment. One of the panelists was registering his disapproval of the death penalty under any circumstances when a listener called to ask, "How would you feel if eight of your daughters were murdered?"

I admired the panelist for his integrity. "In that case," he admitted, "I would be in favor of execution."

This brings us to the Howard Pornographic Principle, developed from observation over a period of many years:

THE FURTHER ONE IS REMOVED FROM
REAL PORNOGRAPHY, THE MORE
PERMISSIVE HE IS LIKELY TO BE.

Thus, a great many psychologists, psychiatrists, and political and social theorists doubt the harmful effect of suggestive literature. They use such phrases as *salutary emotional outlet, safety valve,* and *mental catharsis.*

But among the less doctrinaire and more down-to-earth—those who work directly with youngsters—the attitude is quite the reverse. Policemen who take the stuff from the pockets of young sex offenders are not likely to give out with that *catharsis* business. I have never heard of a single juvenile court judge who would buy the *salutary emotional outlet* line of thinking. Wardens won't allow indecent literature; directors of summer camps forbid it; coaches and athletic directors and scoutmasters don't want it around; army chaplains worry about it; school principals fear it. They must have reasons.

J. Edgar Hoover's reasons are crystal clear:

> *Police officials . . . unequivocally state
> that lewd and obscene material plays a
> motivating role in sexual violence. In case
> after case, the sex criminal has on his per-
> son or in his possession pornographic lit-
> erature or pictures . . . . Such filth in the
> hands of young people and curious adoles-
> cents does untold damage and leads to
> disastrous consequences.*

Those are powerful words. Read them again. But before we get too excited about the dirty book business, maybe we should pursue the big question:

Can mere words and pictures really influence any-body's conduct?

Let me present the Communist nations as Witness No. 1.

The Commies are the world's greatest realists. They *know* the debilitating effect of verbal garbage. One of their standard moves in the softening-up process which precedes every takeover is flooding the country to be taken over with salacious literature. Check with the Czechs.

Witness No. 2: The billion dollar Advertising Industry. Hard-nosed merchandisers and manufacturers, who wouldn't give their grandmother a plug of tobacco if she were dying, scrutinize performance studies before spending millions to put their products in the public eye. A combination of words and pictures convinced women by the millions that it was chic to smoke, and the same combination is now slowly getting some of them to stop. It was the power of the phrase that influenced countless citizens to *Say It with Flowers, Fly the Friendly Skies of United, Bathe with Gentle Ivory, Vote for Kennedy, Brush with Pepsodent, Come Out to Beautiful Wrigley Field and Watch the Cubs Play Ball, Join the Pepsi Generation.*

Words can do wondrous things. They have caused sinners to repent, and lovers to relent. Words can make a blind person "see" a sunset. Words have been known to make a Coolidge laugh, or a woman change her mind, or a big man cry. Words can defeat a Supreme Court nomination, get a football coach fired, attract contributions to the Alumni Fund, rouse people to raise petunias, get married, jog two miles before breakfast, go on the wagon, climb Everest, descend to the ocean floor, run to the refrigerator for a beer, or slice *Faultless* golf balls into the woods.

Some people have a way with words. I look up and see only the ceiling of the universe; Shakespeare peeks at the same sky from the side of the angels and notes "the floor of heaven." One guy writes "Dear Jane;" another says "Jane dear." A reporter sends in a squib about seeing a first-robin of the spring; a more enterprising one tells how a redbreast got a surprise view of a man walking through the woods on a February afternoon. One headline writer can't fit in the details of a jet's being commandeered; another invents the single descriptive term *skyjack.*

Is it unreasonable to argue, then, that if a devotional work can inspire, the works of de Sade can degrade? If a medium can sell Cadillacs to a man, can it not peddle contraceptives to his son? If a biography can make a youngster want to be a Mickey Mantle or a Tom Dooley, can it not also make him aspire to be a Casanova or a Jack the Ripper? If a masterpiece of art can bring a lump to the throat, couldn't a different picture produce a different reaction?

It is one thing to be convinced that pornography warps young minds; it's another thing to do something about it.

For six years I served as Executive Director of the National Office for Decent Literature, an organization formed in 1938 by the Catholic bishops of America to take a look at what they believed was an alarming menace to youth. I was a pallbearer at NODL's funeral on December 31, 1969, and came away from graveside with a few tears and a few convictions:

1. The cloak of anonymity must not be allowed to hang in the closet of smut. Would the food and drug administration allow a manufacturer to put out a drug anonymously? Would Rembrandt issue an unsigned painting? Can anyone imagine the collective screech of the housewives of America if, for just one week, all brand names were

wiped out at the supermart?

Yet tons of irresponsible filth rolls off the presses every month, protected by editorial masquerade. Stephen Lovelady, writing in the *Wall Street Journal* about authors who grind out suggestive novels, reports that "without exception, such craftsmen, who usually earn $500 to $800 a book, employ a pen name."

If a book is so bad that its author is ashamed of it, it should be given the same treatment a newspaper gives an anonymous letter. This isn't censorship; this is just common sense. Readers who wish to remind me that Dr. X was a *nom de plume* and that *Beowulf* and *The Song of Roland* are anonymous may write in care of the publisher.

2. Along the same line, pictures in questionable taste should bear the name of the model and the photographer. If they argue that they are producing great art, let them proudly proclaim their work.

3. Those who have the greatest stake in literature—and the most to lose from

the cheap, tainted, unprofessional publications which threaten to engulf the
newsstands—are the hundreds of legitimate publishers. These houses, which
spend small fortunes confirming the
authenticity, historicity, and statistics
in their manuscripts, could add dignity
and stature to their profession by
adopting a common code and proudly
putting their seal on every publication
which meets the adopted standards. I
cannot conceive of a single subject
which need be taboo. It is merely when
the *treatment* of such subjects is done
purely to rouse prurient interests that
a little self-policing could do a world
of good.

4. John Patrick Public ought to be just
as interested in a Supreme Court nominee's record on obscenity decisions as
he is in the nominee's civil rights record or his labor decisions.

Decency is well rid of Mr. Justice
Fortas. Decency may not be able to
survive another Douglas or Black sit-
ting on the High Court. If John Patrick
is interested in reasonably clean newsstands for his children, he had better

learn to write more and better letters to his U.S. Senators than do the publishers, the smut writers, the Merchants of Menace, and the ACLU.

5. Speaking of the American Civil Liberties Union, I only wish the forces of Decency had the same spirit of dedication. Better yet, I wish the ACLU were on our side, because these boys really dig. In my opinion, some people are a lot more equal than others in ACLU philosophy. How many briefs did the ACLU file in favor of students who were deprived of one or two months education by the Kent-inspired school shutdowns of May, 1970? When the constitutional rights of many firms to recruit on college campuses were forcibly denied in the spring of 1970, where was the American Civil Liberties Union? When students who wished to apply for jobs with these companies were not allowed to do so, did the ACLU exhibit the same burning, passionate concern they have shown on behalf of those who grind out gutter pornography? They did not.

A student at DePaul University attempted in a mas

ters thesis to discover why adults attended evening classes. She mailed out dozens of questionnaires. One nun answered "Holy obedience." And that's how I got into this obscenity business—Holy Obedience. I was enjoying myself as a reasonably carefree assistant pastor, playing a little golf, getting away for an occasional vacation or fishing trip when the assignment came from Cardinal Meyer to take over as Director of the National Office for Decent Literature, headquartered in Chicago's Loop.

Priests are by nature usually aligned with the forces of virtue, so I suppose I was always opposed in principle to obscenity. But it had always been from a convenient left-field bleacher perspective. Now, here I was, a soldier who scarcely knew what the enemy looked like and wouldn't know how to shoot at him anyway. By the time Holy Obedience put me into the act, the mode of operation had been pretty well established, and I did little to change it.

I was many months on the job before I fully realized what a practical, common-sense approach had been worked out by my predecessors. It was pure luck that I found myself involved in a program to which I could enthusiastically subscribe. NODL's philosophy was beautiful; it was constitutional; it was practical. I recommend it whole-heartedly to communities really concerned with the pollution of young, impressionable minds. Nevertheless, NODL was an artistic failure—a bomb, in today's lingo. With a bigger budget, with a little more enthusiasm, with a little applause from a more sensitive Supreme

Court, with a little more dedication of the ACLU type, things might have been different.

What was the NODL philosophy? First of all, we didn't worry about what adults were reading; our concern was with youngsters. The Merchants of Menace are always talking about constitutional rights. NODL concerned itself with the constitutional rights of millions of parents who spend fortunes in time, love, and money to bring up their children in a wholesome, moral climate, only to be thwarted by unconscionable peddlers of latrine literature, basking under the broad umbrella of the First Amendment. In this high noon of Constitutionalism where we lock up the jury and send the defendant home at night, the Constitution has found some most unusual supporters.

Sound melodramatic? Or maybe even a little monsignoric?

If you think I'm overstating the case, try me out. Go out and buy a piece of pornography and show it to the first 20 parents who happen to pass your house. Don't get involved in doctrinaire discussions about free speech and freedom of the press. Simply *show that piece of pornography* to those 20 parents and ask them if they would approve of their youngsters reading it. It's the old Howard Pornographic Principle at work. It's the anti-capital-punishment advocate opening his front door and finding the slain bodies of eight daughters. The forces of Decency could win 4,999,990 front-line soldiers if 5,-000,000 parents could see their children snickering over a piece of real pornography. That *healthy emotional out-*

let and *safety valve* nonsense might occasionally be right, but don't try to pass it off on a worried mother who has been pacing the floor two hours after curfew, and who has just found a slice of raw pornography in her teen-ager's closet.

NODL believed that it was important that youngsters get that good early start. We worked on the principle that the corner drug store and newsstand were far greater factors in kids' lives than the big downtown bookstores. We worked on the principle that if a neighborhood merchant is displaying nylons that run or candy that is sugary or eggs that aren't candled or shirts that won't launder, he ought to be told about it.

We published a monthly list of mass-market paperbacks (youngsters are not likely to buy the egghead stuff or expensive clothbound titles) which, in the opinion of our review board, were "objectionable for youth." That's all—"in our opinion, objectionable for youth." We never used the words "obscene" or "pornographic," whose definitions wavered wondrously in the heyday of the Warren court.

Our workers, usually residents of the neighborhood, made their objections known to drug store and newsstand proprietors. NODL never sanctioned a boycott, never approved of threats. We found that most reputable merchants were delighted to cooperate. They realized that the type of literature we objected to was like an engraved invitation to the black-leather-jacket hangers-on; they found that with these books and magazines there was a high incidence of theft, for many people who could afford to buy them were ashamed to do so. Many looked upon our crusade as a valuable service, for these businessmen did not have time to examine individual titles selected by the wholesale distributor. Once the distributor found that questionable titles were being returned, the selection became more selective. Most important of all, these businessmen had an investment in the neighborhood. They were out to build good will. There are thousands of them ready to cooperate any time somebody asks them.

Among national chains who heartily subscribed to our monthly NODL *Newsletter* and to our philosophy were Walgreen's and Rexall. After a year in which Walgreen's 527 stores refused to sell objectionable titles— even the widely publicized blockbusters—paperback sales *increased* 26% and magazine sales, 10%. The Jack Eckerd chain of 54 Florida drugstores was another of our enthusiastic supporters. All three chains operated on the principle that they could not, in conscience, sell prescriptions and health medicines at one counter and dirty books, "goof pills of the mind," at another counter.

NODL succeeded wherever its people worked, which obviously wasn't often enough. Its principles will operate remarkably well in any community which has made up its corporate mind that it can do without the indignity of printed pollution.

NODL offered its services to people and organizations of all faiths, and our greatest little victories were scored when the campaign was non-sectarian. Indecent literature is the heroin of the spirit, and erodes the souls of young Protestants, Jews, Moslems, atheists and agnostics just as much as it affects young Catholics. Quite often these triumphs were temporary, for volunteers don't get paid, and distributors and their truck drivers do. Eternal vigilance is the price a community must pay for newsstand decency. It's a pretty steep price these days.

NODL was not merely "destructive," to use a term of one of our many detractors. We also had a positive program. Each *Newsletter* listed a few recommended titles among the new paperback releases, and we particularly liked to keep our subscribers aware of the many fine juvenile series. Our lieutenants would show this list to the news vendors, and our supporters went out of their way to buy these titles and to compliment the proprietor on his fine selection. We also sparked projects which stocked reading rooms of some juvenile homes with fresh, wholesome novels.

Of the abominations foisted upon the reading public, it is my opinion that the variety known as the National Tabloid is perhaps the cheapest, the sickest, the crudest, and the cruelest of all.

The tabloid weed thrives in ghetto ground. Here its contents are devoured, unseasoned by a tempering grain of salt, by highly impressionable, semi-literate youngsters and thrill-seekers looking for a quick literary fix at 15¢ and 25¢ a shot. But the National Tabloid is a hardy plant, equally capable of sprouting in the fertile topsoil of suburbia, on Park Avenue, or on Nob Hill. While juvenile crime rates soar, while incidences of drug addiction and venereal disease rise among the young, this typographical pollutant which thrives on stale news, come-into-my-parlor advertising, sensationalized headlines, and sensational photography, goes unchecked on thousands of newsstands. The genus tabloid is too tepid to be pornography, too tawdry to merit critical notice, too ridiculous to be taken seriously by anybody except the poor, pitiful people hooked by its headlines.

Tabloids generally do not subscribe to the nationally recognized news services. Their reports bear no datelines, but employ such chronologically indeterminate phrases as *last week,* or *this summer* or *last year.* Their news sources are cloaked in blessed, libel-free anonymity, typified by such phrases as *authorities said, it is believed, observed a police official, ironically, said one high ranking officer,* and *reliable sources are certain that they'll be convicted and probably executed.* Identification of people is seldom more specific than *a Newark prostitute, a Detroit peep-show proprietor,* or *a St. Louis housewife.*

Tabloid headlines scream EATS MATE ALIVE, while the accompanying news story tells of the predatory diet of a spider; through their columns a reader can obtain *Ten Lessons in Sex Technique* revealing *Every procedure, step-by-step, how to attain full rapturous satisfaction and superb delights of love and sex in all its forms.* From their classified Friendship Marts, the curious can get in touch with *Michigan Marmalade, 37: Tangy-tawny charmer with brown hair, dark eyes, beautiful buxom build,* (*who*) *seeks any race man,* or *Alabama Sociable, 27: Black hair, brown eyes, 5'6", 160 full-busted lbs., Catholic,* (*who*) *will accept kind man of any race.*

Of course, no youngster could possibly obtain advertised material because the coupon which he must sign
asserts: "I am over 21."

Next to the Tabloids, the item which most discour-
aged us at NODL was the unending series of pernicious
novels which monthly sprang from the literary cesspools
operated by such publishers as *Bee-Line, Midwood, Soft-
cover, Wizard* and numerous others. Lesbianism is perhaps the favorite topic; but male homosexuality, wife-
swapping, voyeurism, and fetishism, clinically and allur-
ingly described, are not far behind. We call these paperbacks SHADOWS, maybe because they deal with whispery
subjects and are produced by phantom publishers and
written by authors who hide behind nom de plumes.

The National Tabloids and the Shadows stand as
monoments to the stupidity of a society which is willing
to raft its youngsters down the slough of delinquency
just to keep the boat of Free Speech in the harbor. The
slick, suggestive cover poses and their accompanying
Shadowy titles—*Between Two Men, Interplay, Spanking
—Sex or Sadism*— and the Tabloid headlines—*Tries to
Rape His Sexy Sis*—are cruel monuments to the imprac-
ticability of the Douglas-Black-ACLU philosophy of
everything goes. It is a dirty trick on Thomas Jefferson
and James Madison, who never dreamed of any constitutional protection for this kind of stuff. It's a vicious
thing to do to youngsters whose minds are not yet mature.

The tired old arguments against some semblance of
newsstand responsibility are still filed in the top desk

drawer of the Merchants of Menace. They are:

1. Dirty books never hurt anybody. Probably 98% of the outstanding citizens of our country have been subjected to them, yet they came out all right.

ANSWER: Pornography *does* affect some people. Think of the loss to society if even ONE of a thousand readers is drawn over the threshhold of promiscuity, perversion, crime, or violence.

2. No causal connection between crime and pornography has ever been proven.

ANSWER: Of course not. To do a valid scientific study among youngsters, a representative group of children would have to be enlisted, half of whom would have to be subjected to great gobs of pornography over a long period of time. No parent, however depraved, would ever allow his child to participate in such a study.

3. Where are we going to draw the line? Pretty soon you would be blue-penciling Socrates who wrote of incest, bowdlerizing Shakespeare who got pretty sexy, and even censoring the Bible.

ANSWER: Ridiculous! A few common sense rules are all we need.

So, Mr. Editor, in your *Censorship: For and Against,* put me down with the Againsts. I have talked and corresponded with too many mothers and fathers whose children have been adversely affected by suggestive reading material. I have seen the scrubby little "adult reading centers" which pockmark 42nd Street like ugly ulcers and which are a disgrace to millions of decent passersby. I have read the inside story of the Moors murder case, the most bestial crime in English history, committed by a couple who owned a trunkload of latrine literature.

I have seen the incredibly vicious, vomitous stuff which is making capitalists (and rugged constitutionalists) of a few thousand at the expense of a few million.

I have been to juvenile court.

I can't forget the words of the man who has had more experience with crime and criminals than any man in the United States:

> *In case after case, the sex criminal has on his person or in his possession pornographic literature or pictures. . . . Indecent literature is making criminals faster than we can build jails to house them.*

The first thing one should know about Judith Crist is that she is mad about movies, not at them. She is hated and adored, albeit from different quarters, for the same reason: she calls the shots exactly as she sees them, immune to pressures from any source. She is not only honest—she is blunt. That she can analyze this liveliest of the arts objectively and in depth, with clear intelligence, and also be free of smug estheticism or cultish snobbery accounts in part for her large following.

Since 1963 she has been a film and drama commentator of the NBC-TV Today Show, and is also currently active as film critic for TV GUIDE *and* NEW YORK *magazine.*

She has received a spate of awards. In 1970, she was chosen as one of twelve alumnae to receive the Hunter College President's Medal for distinguished service—the highest award the college may bestow on it alumni.

A poll conducted by Louis Harris Associates found her regarded as the most influential film critic in the United States.

Judith Crist

AT THE MOMENT, the lady has lots of company and a good share of it is in high places. The lady is the one who, so the oldie goes, has phoned the police to arrest the man across the way standing around stark and staring and naked. An officer arrived but could see no one. "He's right there, officer. Just climb up on this chair, and scrunch around the window frame, and hang over a little, and you can see him."

The lady, bolstered by a Vice-Presidential declaration that "so long as Richard Nixon is President, Main Street is not going to turn into Smut Alley," is now in the forefront of the latest howl for censorship. We are experiencing the thoroughly expected and not unnatural backlash against the changing mores of the last half of the Sixties. Once again we have completed a social cycle and a social circle that has left the unperceptive with present shock. Normal progressions, accelerated beyond the speed of sight in this age of instant communication, have exploded with terrifying force. And unless the voices of sanity are ready with a reply, we may well be on the brink of the censorious Seventies—a period of retrogression that would negate the astonishing advances toward intellectual honesty and creative freedom that we have made in recent years.

These advances are not blatantly evident to the eye.

But consider what an exile from this country in the Sixties would note on his return in 1970. Kurt Vonnegut Jr.'s Looseleaf, returning after eight lost years with the Ulysses-like hero of *Happy Birthday, Wanda June,* observes, "You know what gets me—how all the magazines show tits today. Used to be against the law, didn't it? Must have changed the law. . . . You know what gets me—how everybody says *fuck* and *shit* all the time now. I used to be scared shitless I'd say *fuck* or *shit* in public by accident. Now everybody says *fuck* and *shit* all the time. Something very big must have happened while we were out of the country. . . . You know what gets me—how short the skirts are. Something very important about sex must have happened while we were gone . . ."

What happened about sex in the Sixties was simply a matter of economics and evolution as far as stage and screen and literature were concerned: a coming of age, a realism in understanding our mores, and a new freedom in the arts. There were the landmark court rulings on obscenity, the frenetic fumbling of the film industry at self-regulation, the fading of local censors, the opening of the floodgates for the exploiters, the all-too-human confusion of freedom with license—and then shock at how far we'd come so soon. From the sealed-lips coolth of Hollywood kisses, we were plunged into a wallow of hip and thigh and genitalia; from the over-dressed stage extravaganza, we were down to nudes cavorting, to smutty stories and to social statements. From the bang-bang-you're-dead of off-screen sound-effect violence, we were soaking in full-color blood baths on a small screen in our very homes.

Clark Gable's "Frankly, my dear, I don't give a damn," hard-won from the industry's censors by David Selznick in 1939, had in fewer than 30 years faded before a stream of four-, five- and seven-letter obscenities from the lovely lips of Elizabeth Taylor. Though right up to the Sixties Hollywood insisted on stuffing a jewel into the meanest belly dancer's belly button, by the Seventies there hadn't been a part of the human anatomy that had not been fully displayed on the big screen, and the amount of pubic hair on show became the industry's standard for deciding whether a teen-ager could see a film under parental escort or not at all.

At least, the startled homefolks remarked, they would not be seeing this sort of thing in the privacy of their own homes (where nudity, one gathers from the morality mavens, is strictly taboo). But by the 1970-71 television season, those very R-rated films (requiring parental escore) were being shown virtually intact on the telly; and a couple of cause celebres of the early Sixties, *Hurry Sundown* (with a phallic saxaphone scene that had deeply upset the Catholics) and *The World of Suzy Wong* (a eulogy to the virtues of a Hong Kong whore from which Grauman's Chinese had barred unescorted sub-sixteeners) were telecast intact—and in prime network time yet!

All of this seems to have happened overnight, particularly in my own medium of film, where the occasional moviegoer, so long wrapped in the cottonwool of the film industry's moral hypocrisy, has experienced a decade of constant trauma. We tend to cling, first, to our peculiar puritanisms: deny the flesh with shame for the beauty of the body and permission only to watch its desecration and destruction as payment for sin. Secondly, we still believe in the mass-entertainment escapism function of the commercial films of 30 and 40 years ago. Many still think of movies as mass-manufactured fodder for the national 12-year-old mentality that filmdom ascribed to all ages. Few are fully aware of the economic revolution that has brought the independent film maker and the auteur to the forefront with personal films for individuals and special interest groups. Thus, sporadic visits to the changing film scene are unnerving even to the sophisticate. And a professional moviegoer like myself is hard put to remember that it was only ten years ago—and not in another lifetime—that we were goosefleshed by the realization that the undulating shadows at the outset of *Hiroshima, Mon Amour* were naked bodies in embrace. Today, the screen-watching workday is a rare one that has not provided a minimum of three orgasms by noon, plus a goodly detailing of sadism, masochism, homosexuality and mayhem by quitting time.

And for the eroticized enthusiast beyond the "respectable" movie houses, there are the mini-movies showing their stag and blue movies, the peep shows, the porno-photo shops, and the so-called movie-making establishments where patrons can watch the alleged filming of skin-flicks. The day of the exploiter is at hand. The bestseller lists are topped by how-to sex books, and the theaters are flooded with how-to sex movies. Much in the manner of the Hollywood Biblical which wallowed in dancing girls and violence and romance with the Good Book as its alibi, so the sexploitation flick pretends to be "document-ing" the state of pornography abroad, or "educating" the inept at refinements of erotica for marital bliss, or "telling it how it is"—with a warning, of course, that lechery, like crime, doesn't pay for anyone but the smut-film maker.

Small wonder, then, that the cry for censorship had arisen in the late Sixties, and has come to a scream with the ultimate libertarianism of the President's Commission on Obscenity and Pornography whose findings were made public in October, 1970. The majority finding, that there was "no warrant for continued governmental interference with the full freedom of adults to read, obtain or view" pornographic materials, confirmed the know-nothing sus-picion that the fall into the slimepit was indeed at hand.

Well, not quite. A variety of Congressional commit-tees probing sex and violence in films and on television were still to be heard from. And simultaneously, a New York Criminal Courts judge held that *Censorship in Den-mark,* a documentary that detailed Copenhagen's pornog-raphy fair for those who couldn't take the sightseeing trip for themselves, was "patently offensive to most Americans because it affronts community standards relating to the description or representation of sexual matters," and had, as its dominant theme, "a prurient interest in sex."

But the point, of course, to the consideration of censorship I am edging toward, is simply that "most Americans" are under no obligation to affront themselves by going to see *Censorship in Denmark*. They are free to exercise the only kind of censorship in which I wholeheartedly believe: self-censorship on the part of the public and, hopefully, on the part of the creator. And it is on behalf of the minority of Americans who would only not be affronted but also might be edified, or enlightened, or simply titillated by this movie that we must fight for the freedom of film.

Before we go further into what is essentially a consideration of a film and theater critic's view of censorship, I should note that far more qualified professionals—lawyers, psychologists, behavioralists, sociologists—have explored the field to a fare-thee-well. No layman could hone the legalisms as brilliantly as has Charles Rembar in *The End of Obscenity,* recounting his triumphant defenses of the publications of *Lady Chatterley, Tropic of Cancer* and *Fanny Hill,* nor as Ephraim London has in his various defenses of films, from the 1952 case of *The Miracle* which established the film as a medium rather than an industry, and, most important, as a medium and an art form entitled to the protection of the First Amendment. It was Mr. London who, at the very time the New York City police were picking up *Censorship in Denmark,* won a reversal from the United States Court of Appeals of a judgment by a lower Federal Court approving a Customs confiscation of a Swedish film *Language of Love.* I think the opinion, written for the three-man court by Circuit

Judge Leonard Moore, is worth quoting in part, both for its urbanity and its principle. He describes the film as:

> *a movie version of the 'marriage manual'* *—that ubiquitous panacea (in the view of some) for all that ails modern man-woman relations.*
>
> *Assuming the Masters and Johnson* (HUMAN SEXUAL RESPONSE, 1966) *premise that the path to marital euphoria and social utopia lies in the perfection and practice of clinically correct and complete sexual technology, this film offers to light that path in a way the masses can understand. It purports to be an animated Little Golden Book of marital relations, or perhaps the KAMA SUTRA of electronic media, although the film is nowhere nearly as rich in the variety of its smorgasbord of delights as comparison with that ancient Hindu classic might suggest. It may be the vulgate scripture, the Popular Mechanics of interpersonal relations, the complete cure for the ailing marriage. Or so goes the theory of its sponsors.*
>
> LANGUAGE OF LOVE *stars four of what are apparently leading Scandinavian sexual technocrats, with brilliant cameo roles for the functioning flesh of various un-*

> *named actors. . . . This film, as did* I AM
> CURIOUS (YELLOW), *contains scenes of
> oral-genital contact and other hetero-
> sexual activity that no actor or actress
> would ever have confessed knowledge of
> in bygone days of the silver screen. Never-
> theless, the movie-going public has been
> confronted with all of this before in recent
> times.*

Viewing the film in its "tedious entirety," Judge
Moore held it not proscribably obscene on established
constitutional tests, but noted frankly that the court found
several sequences offensive:

> *not because they excited predilections to
> prurience but because they intruded upon
> areas of interpersonal relations which we
> consider to be peculiarly private. Our
> sensibilities were offended, but that is a
> matter of taste and de gustibus non est
> disputandum, particularly in matters of
> sex and constitutional law.*

Granted that certain scenes might have erotic appeal
to the average person, the court observed, "Indeed erotic
appeal has assumed a position of paramount importance,
somewhat overemphasized we think, in the affairs of our
daily lives," but it is not to be equated with "prurient interest." Simplistic or superficial, tedious or over-clinical

though the discussion of sex might be, the film, the court found, had redeeming social value in its advocacy of ideas.

The court asked:

> *In final analysis is freedom of speech and expression, including exhibition of motion picture films, to be based on the opinions of 51 percent or even 80 percent of our populace? If so, it might well be that on a national plebiscite the* LANGUAGE OF LOVE, I AM CURIOUS (YELLOW), LES AMANTS, MEMOIRS OF A WOMAN OF PLEASURE (FANNY HILL) *and others would all be condemned by a majority vote. Minorities would then read and see what their fellow men would decide to permit them to read and see. The shadow of 1984 would indeed be commencing to darken our horizon. . . . .*

The court concluded:

> *Whether these decisions will bring forth a more enlightened people who have lived long under sex taboos or will cause a moral degredation of the race will be for the historian . . .*

Certainly, a film historian will find an enlightened public feasting off any number of fine films of the past decade that were made possible by a relaxation of taboos. *Hiroshima, Mon Amour, The Virgin Spring, The Apartment, Elmer Gantry, The Hustler, Two Women, Divorce—Italian Style, Tom Jones, 8½, Hud, Dr. Strangelove, The Servant, Darling, Mickey One, Georgy Girl, Bonnie and Clyde, Ulysses, The Graduate, The Killing of Sister George, Last Summer, Midnight Cowboy, Women in Love, The Virgin and the Gypsy, Five Easy Pieces, Putney Swope, Going Down the Road, Brewster McCloud, Little Murders* are but a few of the films of quality that would not have been made, let alone shown to us intact, had there not been a steady erosion of censorship.

The idiocies of film censorship up to 1964 are nowhere better documented than by Murray Schumach in *The Face on the Cutting Room Floor*. He ended his chronicle as the industry was preparing for self-regulation, with a certain optimism. Had the industry settled for a simple not-for-children classification, the system might have functioned on less farcical terms than it has. The ratings start with *G*, which means for general consumption; *M*, stands for "mature," a rating abandoned (possibly on the realization that few movies could deserve that label) in favor of *GP*, which stands for general consumption but parental discretion advised; *R*, which restricts teen-agers to admission with parental or guardian escort, and *X*. This last designation was intended to signify adult admission only, but of course, is considered the label of the dirty movie—either to be capitalized on by the smut-men or sought out by the prurient or to be ostracized by theater managements and newspaper advertising pages catering to the bluenoses.

The politicking and juggling and bargaining over the gradations of rating has been shocking, with moviegoers misled and children misguided and the independent and minor moviemaker getting short shrift and little consideration in the rating game. In the same way, the little man has suffered from the censor; fighting a case from police precinct to the Supreme Court is a costly process and, as a result, not a democratic one.

Beyond the film historian, the sociologist and the psychologist have endlessly debated in slick magazines and learned journals whether the moral degradation of the race is upon us. There is mountainous material— none of it definitive—to prove that sex and violence are harmless and/or harmful for the young. For my part, I wish there were as much concern about shielding them from the destructive forces of real life as there is about the possible effects a film or a television show may have upon their little psyches. Children, I have found, are particularly resilient in this audio-visual age; they are no longer naive, as my generation was, about the fictional creations of film. My worry, in fact, is that they are so sophisticated about the manufacture of their entertainments that they even suspect the reality of the riots and battles they see on the news shows, half-expecting the skull-smashed demonstrator and the shattered Vietnamese soldier to wash off the makeup and show up on a game show the next day. But children should be protected from the ugliness, the inhumanity, the grostesque distortions of hard-core pornography, just as they should be protected from the sadism, the perversity, and the disregard of human values in the violent entertainments presented to them in the guise of adventure shows. This is, of course, a parental responsibility; but parents—like booksellers, theater owners, producers, and distributors—may well decline their moral responsibilities. The realist must, I fear, demand some legal restrictions where minors are concerned.

But the American adult must take responsibility for himself, with the right to exercise his own standards. The ones who shout the loudest about being "swamped" and "flooded" with filth via the mails—I often wonder why our mailbox is never defiled by even a dribble—seem never to exercise their privilege of throwing brochures away unread, twisting the dial, or heaven help us, turning off the set, or simply not going into a suspect movie. And the ones who worry most about the children are for the most part bachelors or spinsters who haven't done a day's social service in their lives, beyond, perhaps, joining a police action against a film.

I became aware of this state of affairs from the stream of police witnesses in the case against *The Killing of Sister George* in Boston, where witness after witness testified to forcing himself or herself to sit through the whole film to the near-final two-minute breast-nibbling scene between two women—all for the sake of the children they did not have. And nowhere was there anyone to contradict the exhibitor's contention that no one under the age of eighteen had been admitted to the film.

And what possible ill effect, beyond boredom, could the film or scene have had upon children? In this age of bottle-babies, I doubt that a five-year-old would have had even nostalgic yearnings in the course of the scene. Only the most naive or prudish adult might have been "offended"—but he, of course, was not obliged to attend.

Beyond the effects of violence and sex on children, the social scientists have made endless studies of the effects of pornography on crime and other anti-social actions. Again, so long as the Danes' experience has not been totally researched, the findings can be used on either side.

I remain convinced that no female has been raped by text or film and that the triggering of the psychotic mind cannot be predetermined or even pin-pointed.

I do know, however, what censorship accomplishes, creating an unreal and hypocritical mythology, formenting an attraction for forbidden fruit, inhibiting the creative minds among us and fostering an illicit trade. Above all, it curtails the right of the individual, be he creator or consumer, to satisfy his intellect and his interest without harm. In our law-rooted society, we are not the keeper of our brother's morals—only of his rights.

In protecting those rights we must be Voltairean, advocating, as Holmes said, "not free thought for those who agree with us, but freedom for the thought that we hate." It's a good principle, but I must confess that I declined to testify on behalf of *I Am Curious (Yellow)* and *Language of Love*. I claimed the critic's privilege, if not the civil libertarian's, of choosing to advocate beyond pure principle on aesthetic grounds. If other critics had not been found to testify, I would have done my service—but one wearies of going to the barricades to fight for trash. I did testify on behalf of *Sister George,* a remarkably fine film, and for *491,* an earlier work by the director of *I Am Curious,* that was distinguished by honest aspiration and artistry. But my irritation with and optional withdrawal from the legalistic battles were directed purely at the censors, at the U.S. Customs officials and petty police (servants, alas, of small-minded bigoted citizens) who were completely negating their avowed purpose. Had *Curious (Yellow)* not become a cause celebre, it would have opened in a small art house in New York and suffered a quiet death from negative criticism and word-of-mouth. Instead, misguided but well-intentioned critics took up the cause, its ersatz sexuality was highly publicized and its shrewd importers made millions from a voyeuristic public. Even with *Sister George* the Boston police doubled-crossed themselves. They seized the film but had to release it immediately under an anti-prior-restraint injunction; the film had been doing good business up to then but zoomed into smash-hit status while the publicized censorship battle was fought.

It's not just the censors who publicize smut. The smart exhibitor in recent years has even capitalized on the censorious critic. The banner quote-line exploited at a theater's showing of Ingmar Bergman's *The Silence* back in 1964 was a lady critic's "This is the dirtiest movie I've ever seen!" and the leather jackets went pouring in, only to find themselves completely frustrated in their attempts to recognize the highly touted masturbation, intercourse, and cunnilingus scenes that the censors had debated but which Bergman's artistry hid from the pornography-minded. But let's not be snobbish. A Michigan State film society recently touted a revival of *The Ape Woman* by quoting me as deeming it "the depth of unappetizing movie making."

Well, the depths have been plumbed a lot deeper since that 1964 film and moviegoers are now assured that they will tremble, throw up and sweat at the ecstasies and horrors to be seen within. But we are, I suspect, reaching the end of the era of voyeurism. We have seen it all and are ready to put it in perspective. The blue-movie audience (long ago composed of the wealthy dilletante or the frat boys or the fellows at the firehouse) is made up largely of middle-aged businessmen and oldsters. The younger generation has either been there, legitimately, and taken it in stride—or couldn't care less.

One goes back to the days of one's youth, of pouring over pages 723ff in the Modern Library edition of *Ulysses,* of gulping down snatches of *Lady Chatterley* in a bootlegged brown-paper-bound edition, and of going from there into the twin-bedded cinematic world of Doris Day's eternal virginity.

The other day I came home to find my fourteen-year-old finishing *Tropic of Cancer*. "Boy, what a bore!" he remarked, tossing the book aside. And beyond his qualifications as a literary critic, I think him a healthier type than my contemporaries. So much, then, for the moral decline of the race.

Carey McWilliams has been in the forefront of liberal movements for many decades. He is best known as editor of THE NATION, *a position he has held since 1955.*

Born in Colorado, Mr. McWilliams was graduated from the University of Southern California. He is the author of a number of books, including AMBROSE BIERCE: A BIOGRAPHY, BROTHERS UNDER THE SKIN, PREJUDICE, A MASK FOR PRIVILEGE *and* WITCH: THE REVIVAL OF HERESY.

Carey McWilliams

THE PARADOX ABOUT CENSORSHIP is that everyone is opposed to it—literally everyone. If proof be needed, just try to censure a censor.

The idea of censorship is inherently repugnant to most Americans. Asked if they approve of censorship, most of them, as a quick reaction, would say no. But then as they thought about it a bit, some of them would add, "except, of course, in certain situations." The argument about censorship begins with these exceptions—not the general proposition. When the minute exceptions enter the dialogue, the trouble starts.

I am opposed to censorship in all forms, without any exceptions. As a matter of social philosophy, I do not like the idea of some people trying to protect the minds and morals of other people. In practice, this means that a majority seeks to impose its standards on a minority; hence, an element of coercion is inherent in the idea of censorship. In ruling against the ban in Boston on the film *I Am Curious (Yellow)*, Justice Douglas said:

> *I think the First Amendment bars all kinds of censorship. What can be done to literature under the banner of obscenity can be done to other parts of the spectrum of ideas when party or majoritarian*

> *demands mount and propagandists start*
> *declaiming the law.*

I agree.

But since everyone is against censorship as a general proposition, the real argument that must be advanced is the practical argument against the exceptions that are always claimed. Not only do these exceptions, once granted, tend to expand and multiply and eventually to devour the principle, but they have other undesirable practical consequences.

For one thing, ours is a society which places much too heavy a burden on the law as a means of social control. We are "law conscious" and "law minded" to an excessive degree. With us the first reaction to any new social evil is the familiar demand "pass a law." If the evil persists or grows worse, the follow-up response is a demand that law enforcement officials *crack down, get tough, throw the book at them,* etc. And if this doesn't work, then the cry goes forth to amend the law, to make it more sweeping in scope or to increase its penalties. With us these are knee-jerk reactions—we react in this fashion without knowing, or seeking to find out, what it is that causes the evils of which we complain.

It is almost as though we did not believe that evils had causes. Only later, when the "make-it-a-crime" approach has demonstrably failed, do we set up a commission to study the underlying causes; and then, of course, ignore the reports that are eventually issued. One of the reasons—there are others—for our absurd over-reliance on the law as a means of social control is that we are, for the most part, a busy, hard-working people and do not wish to take time out to think about social problems. The pass-a-law reaction is a reflection of our intense preoccupation with individual pursuits, careers, and interests. At the same time we have, as Norval Morris and Gordon Hawkins point out in *An Honest Politician's Guide to Crime Control,* a highly moralistic criminal law and a long tradition of using it as an instrument for coercing men toward virtue. No doubt this stems in part at least from the Puritan legacy. Whatever the cause, we are prone to moralize about social problems. To us "someone is to blame" and must be punished. If enough people can be punished severely enough, we assume the problem—whatever it is—will vanish.

As a consequence of these twin tendencies—an over-reliance on the law as a means of social control and an impulse to use the criminal law to compel men to be virtuous— we have greatly overburdened the courts. Morris and Hawkins estimate that nearly half of the arrests made in the United States have to do not with crimes against persons and property, but with attempts to regulate the moral behavior of individuals. The results are obvious: the calendars of criminal courts are hopelessly congested; trials are long delayed; rehabilitation programs are neglected; and major crimes go unpunished. But faced with these conditions, the most persistent response has been: Build more jails!

In brief, a major cause of the crisis in law enforcement is to be found in our insistence on using the criminal law to attain purposes for which it is not well-suited. We need to remind ourselves that the law is, at best, a blunt instrumentality. Judges and juries, guided by the wisdom of the common law, can make certain kinds of distinctions and determinations with reasonable competence. But the law is not competent to deal with many matters that we have relegated to it. To free it for the tasks for which it is not only competent but indispensable, we should be withdrawing the excessive burdens we have put on it for which it is not competent.

Censorship is pre-eminently one of these burdens. There is, first of all, the practical difficulty of defining concepts. As the American Civil Liberties Union has pointed out (formal statement, May 11, 1970), such terms as *obscenity* and *pornography* defy definition.

> *They have no meaning other than in terms entirely individual and drawing on each person's religious and moral standards or concepts of good taste.*

What is *obscene* to one person may be merely tiresome to another. Words such as *prurient* and *lascivious* and *lewd* have dictionary definitions, but they cannot be defined with legal precision. Nor can any of these terms be defined in a manner that will prevent the definition from being distorted by local bigots and smut hounds.

But beyond definition is the question of function, of who should judge. The legal process is directed toward securing a verdict; that is the way courts deal with facts. But in debates about values—which is what censorship involves—we insist that the verdict is never in, that no one has the right to close off debate (see article by Fred Haines, *The Nation,* September 14, 1964). What seems a value today may not be regarded as a value tomorrow.

Consider, for example, the difficulties which the Supreme Court has encountered in passing on so-called obscenity legislation. It began with the *Roth* case in 1957 when, for the first time, the Court passed directly on the constitutionality of such legislation. In this case the Court held that "obscenity is not within the area of constitutionally protected speech or press." This may have been historically true but only in the limited sense that state anti-obscenity laws had existed prior to the adoption of the First Amendment. Once this ruling was made, the Court's problems began.

The Supreme Court started out by providing this test of obscenity:

> *Whether to the average person, applying contemporary community standards, the dominant theme of the material taken as a whole appeals to prurient interests.*

This seems like a simple test but the Court began to be plagued with subsequent cases which involved challenging variations. So in 1966, it redefined the test by saying that three elements must coalesce. It must be established that:

1. The dominant theme of the material taken as a whole appeals to a prurient interest in sex;

2. The material is patently offensive because it affronts contemporary community standards relating to the description or representation of sexual matters; and

3. The material is utterly without redeeming social value. (*Memoirs* v. *Massachusetts*, 383 U. S. 413, 1966).

But even this brave effort at definition, achieved after a decade of litigation, scarcely represented a consensus among the members of the Court. In the *Roth* case, there were four separate opinions; in *Memoirs,* there were five separate opinions, with an additional two justices issuing their concurrences based on their opinions in a companion case. In fact the opinion of the Court represented the opinion of only three of nine justices!

By itself this would constitute a judicial nightmare; but in the companion case of *Ginzburg,* four separate opinions affirmed conviction based on violations of the federal obscenity law for mailing three publications. While purporting to adhere to the threefold test enunciated above, the Court, in fact, acknowledged that the publications in question were not utterly without redeeming social value; but it affirmed the convictions anyway. It did so by adding a new element to the test, without specifically saying that this was what it was doing. The added element had reference to the setting in which the publications were presented. These three cases, then, contain in effect 15 separate opinions; and even so, their holdings are, as Judge Edward S. Northrop of the U. S. District Court of Maryland has said, "somewhat ambiguous!" (*Congressional Record,* May 28, 1970, p. E-4832.) In fact, in the ten years prior to 1968, the Supreme Court handed down 13 "obscenity" decisions in which there were 53 separate opinions!

The net result has been, as Elmer Gertz, a distinguished civil liberties lawyer with large experience in censorship cases, has pointed out:

> *The Court has tried in the area of the First Amendment to balance freedom against local pressures and passions, and the local feelings are what survive, except in rare instances when someone can afford the time, expense, wear and tear and uncertainty of carrying his case through the judicial hierarchy to the Supreme Court.*

Experience forced Mr. Gertz to the conclusion that:

> *to permit any limitation on the access to reading was, in practice, to allow all encroachments dictated by local illiterates, bigots and prudes. I found that one can*

> *theorize about the banning of hard-core*
> *pornography, but that in fact the phrase*
> *becomes the excuse for banning, or haras-*
> *sing, everything the less enlightened de-*
> *cry.* (THE NATION, July 5, 1965)

This is, one might say, the natural history of censorship.

Keeping the argument on the purely practical plane, is there then any reason to believe that the condition of which the censors complain would have been any worse had the Supreme Court in 1957 followed the lead of Justice Douglas and interpreted the First Amendment as establishing a total prohibition of censorship? On balance, it seems to me that, by ruling as it did, the Court created an area within which local authorities could act to suppress certain materials, books, films, photographs, and magazines, and that the effect of such action was to advertise the materials in question, thereby enlarging the market and enhancing the price at which such materials could be sold. In brief, the effect of the ruling in the *Roth* and subsequent cases has been to aggravate the condition which the censors *say* they wish to correct. Such, at any rate, seems to be the historical judgment.

C. H. Rolph, after reviewing the British experience, concludes that the trade in so-called obscene and pornographic material "derives a fresh stimulus from every effort to stamp it out by police action." (*Encounter,* June, 1969, p. 23)

Taking the censors at face value, what is the situation of which they complain? The censors contend that there has been a flood of so-called obscene and pornographic material, but they often fail to note that this flood has increased since 1957, i.e., since the *Roth* case. "Erotica has come of age," reports the *Los Angeles Times* (November 3, 1969); Los Angeles is, of course, one of the capitals of the mail-order erotica firms. No one knows exactly just how large this mail-order trade in pornography has become.

Lansing R. Shepard, in the *Christian Science Monitor* (April 18, 1970), makes a minimum estimate of $95 million annually and a maximum gross estimate of $115 million. Whatever the correct figures may be, one can assume: (1) that the trade is large; (2) that it has been growing since 1957; and (3) that it is highly profitable. Prices are high and profit margins are huge. The sale of 20 copies of a "hard-core" pornographic paperback book will net the retailer more than the sale of 250 copies of *Playboy*. Attempts to suppress the trade have only contributed to its profitability and enlarged its volume.

Writes Gerald S. Maltz, former associate editor of the New York *Law Forum,*

> *The big business of pornography thrives on the very laws that impede its supply and increase the demand. Experience has shown that the word 'censored' is more profitable to the pornographer than the content of the material.* (CONGRESSIONAL RECORD, May 1, 1970, p. E-3882)

The censors argue, of course, that while this flood of material might not necessarily corrupt adults, it could have a harmful effect on "young and tender" minds. But the facts show that the overwhelming bulk of such material is purchased by adults, mostly males (Noel Greenwood, *Los Angeles Times,* November 3, 1969). It is essentially an adult market.

Adults, of course, have a habit of exaggerating the extent to which minors may be disturbed by stimuli that disturb them. My experience suggests that the young are interested in what interests them, and not in what adults think might interest them. And the young are not all of one kind. Their interests vary in relation to background, educational levels, degree of sophistication and other factors. By and large the young are resistant to indoctrination by adults and are not as "innocent" or as susceptible to suggestion as adults imagine them to be. As readers of Richard Hughes's *A High Wind in Jamaica* and William Golding's *Lord of the Flies* will probably concede, the young are capable of cruel and insensitive behavior, for which they need no adult stimulus.

The censors also contend, of course, that obscene and pornographic material can have harmful consequences if read by psychologically disturbed adults. But there are simply no acceptable empirical studies by psychiatrists, psychologists, biologists, physiologists, criminologists, statisticians, sociologists, or scientists generally which would indicate a direct relationship between exposure to erotic stimuli and the commission of criminal acts. In fact there is no hard evidence that such exposure has adverse effects on individuals or on society as a whole.

As a matter of fact it has been suggested that erotic books and films may serve an indirect therapeutic purpose by providing an escape hatch or safety valve for the erotic fantasies of disturbed adults. The demand for such material is usually a product of severe repression, strong guilt feelings, intense curiosity, or sexual deprivation. The lonely male drifters who move in and out of the bookstores and cheap movies on 42nd Street in New York are not what they are because of exposure to pornographic material; they are drawn to such material because they *are* lonely men, often with personal problems, without the resources or aptitudes to escape from the dead-end situations in which they find themselves.

Those who feel that prohibiting the sale of obscene material to minors would safeguard their morals should examine what actually happens in such situations. As a police measure, prohibitions against the sale of obscene materials to minors are notoriously ineffective. The dealer may sell the material to an adult who can walk out of the bookstore with impunity and then hand the package to a youngster. At the same time, such ordinances place a most unfair burden on the bookdealer. He must judge the age of the customer at his peril. In fact the volume of material of all kinds is such that it is quite unfair to expect a bookdealer to be familiar with every item on his shelves.

But more to the point, police seldom make arrests in such cases unless they have been instigated to take action by some "League for Pure Books" or similar organization. Usually a complaint is received that a particular bookdealer carries material of this sort and is selling it to minors. The police know how to make arrests in such situations. A youngster is given a marked bill and is told to make a purchase. Using a youngster as a police agent in this manner is hardly likely to increase his respect for the police, or for the law or for the society the police serve. Ordinances prohibiting the sale of such material to minors are never systematically enforced; there are too many sellers and too much material. As a matter of fact, few prosecutions for sales to minors are initiated (see Gertz, above).

Nor should the fact be overlooked that most censorship or anti-smut campaigns are either directed as rackets or conducted for ulterior purposes. The John Birch Society and similar groups have been known to sponsor censorship initiatives as a means of enlisting the support of lower-middle-class elements in right-wing political programs. The connection is not fortuitous. Censorship is a form of repression. The demand for it stems from the same elements that are likely to demand other forms of repression. "Clean book" campaigns are often used as bait to capture the attention of the unsophisticated and the unwary. For example, the initiative campaign conducted by CLEAN in California—California League Enlisting Action Now—had obvious political implications (see article by William Wingfield, "California's Dirty Book Caper," *The Nation*, April 18, 1960).

Taken at face value, the argument of the censors is misdirected. It should be addressed to the interests and institutions responsible for the state of popular culture. Angry parents insist that Congress enact federal anti-obscenity legislation to "protect" their homes and their children. But just how can such parents protect their children against prurient suggestion today? Present-day American society places an inordinate emphasis on sex. The commercialization of sex, as reflected in American advertising, has even become a source of concern to the more responsible Madison Avenue agencies. Some advertising is far more vulgar than the naughtiness of *Fanny Hill* which, incidentally, is largely free of obscene language. Some of the ads in the women's magazines are more vulgar than the sexy photographs and cartoons in *Playboy;* the latter are direct and plain, the former are often cute and suggestive. A peak can be more tantalizing than a good look. *The New York Times Magazine* is replete with ads of beautiful girls in the flimsiest of flimsies. As Justic Douglas has observed, our best magazines are "chockful of thighs, ankles, calves, bosoms, eyes, and hair."

Writes C. H. Rolph:

> *The deliberate excitation of sexual feelings is the purpose of most fashion design, at least for women; of much of the world's greatest art; of the cosmetics industry; and, it appears, of the pictorial advertising for most commodities and services from toothpaste to North Sea gas.*

The banning of sexual symbols from advertising would instantly plunge Madison Avenue into deep despair. The treatment of sex in many best-selling novels, which never fall foul of censorship ordinances, is meant to be prurient although it most often is merely dull. The movies based on these novels are more vulgar than the novels. But this massive accumulation of sex-ridden, sex-drenched material to which children are exposed from an early age, often by their parents, enjoys total immunity from the wrath of the professional censors.

The argument, of course, is often made that the unrestricted circulation of obscene materials operates to break down moral standards by undermining the convictions and sensitivities which support them. To Dr. S. I. Hayakawa, president of San Francisco State College and a semanticist by profession, "the unbridled use of obscenity means a tremendous deterioration in human relations." (*Los Angeles Times,* May 20; 1970.) The inference seems to be that the absence of censorship leads to the widespread circulation of such terms, or that if censorship were invoked it would check such use.

But obscenities, printed or verbal, do not undermine societies; they are more likely to reflect social changes that have been brought about by far more fundamental causes. If popular culture in the United States has cheap and degrading aspects, it may well be that the home, the schools, the universities, the churches and other institutions of the society have failed to provide correctives. It may also be due to the absence of sharp, relevant, and consistent criticism. Rapid social change creates conditions in which insurgent groups, seeking a place in the sun, bring their language, their words, their ways of expressing themselves into the general political dialogue.

The language of some black militants and of some student activists is a case in point. As David Littlejohn of Station KQED in San Francisco has pointed out:

> *Insofar as bellbottoms and sideburns spread, so does everything else. Insofar as soul music becomes background for commercials, these things are catching on by the kind of instant osmosis of the media.*

Given the currency of certain obscenities, he notes, it would be silly to describe a Black Panther rally or a rock festival in school book language. (*Los Angeles Times,* May 20, 1970.) This state of affairs was not brought about by the absence of censorship, nor would censorship correct it.

The fact that there has always been a market of sorts for obscene and pornographic materials suggests that these materials must serve a purpose, of some kind, for some people. In today's mass-market society with today's mass media, more people have access to such materials than in former times. As Christopher Ricks has written (*The Listener,* February 26, 1970):

> *In restoration England, the mob of gentlemen wrote pornography with ease; and in public they stripped and even execrated,*

with something approaching Yippy lav-
ishness.

At one time, pornographic and obscene materials were, as he points out, "the monopoly of gloating biblio-philes," who alone could afford to buy them. Old-line bookstores—as distinguished from today's paperback supermarkets—usually reserved a few choice porno-graphic items, kept under lock and key, for a few rich customers. A leading bookman in San Francisco told me in the late 1920's that one of his steadiest customers for all kinds of erotica was the president of a large university in Los Angeles. Today, as Mr. Ricks points out, "per-missiveness has merely ceased to be a class privilege." All of America is, today, one vast mass market served by the mass media. In such a setting, provincial standards and local customs break down. Family ties are weakened. The influence of the neighborhood church declines. Not surprisingly, there is a mass market, of a sort, for obscene and pornographic materials that were formerly restricted to "gloating bibliophiles" with money. And given the general permissiveness of the society and the influence of the mass media, such materials are more openly dis-played than formerly. But it would be reversing cause and effect to attribute this state of affairs to the absence of censorship.

It is often said, of course, that motion pictures should be regarded in a different category than, say, printed works. The argument is that what might be harmless if read or seen by an individual in the isolation of his study takes on different implications if viewed by a large, diverse audience of both sexes and all ages. But the reverse argument may be nearer the truth, namely that there is a saving grace in numbers; that an open or public presentation before a group has a better chance of producing a balanced judgment. Be this as it may, censorship has a dismal history in the motion picture industry.

In his book, *See No Evil,* Jack Vizzard has told the story of censorship in Hollywood; and it does not make pleasant or reassuring reading. There were overtones of favoritism, conflict-of-interest, influence peddling, and corruption in the former code setup. The present rating system is certainly not ideal, but it seems to work fairly well. True, some producers actually try hard to secure an X rating for a film that is not likely to do well at the box office without it. And it is always possible, by a little doctoring of a script, to secure a general rating without making any fundamental changes in a story.

But the rating system does put the onus on the parent, and on the viewer, and on the public. As Stanley Kramer said recently:

> *The film-maker accepts responsibility for informing the public as to the nature of what he has made. The public accepts responsibility for choosing what it wants to see and for what it wants its children to see. This is as it should be.* (VARIETY, June 11, 1970.)

There are obviously farcical aspects to the rating system; it cannot, for example, insure that there are *any* good films for children to see. But it is certainly preferable to the old-style code censorship.

Of late years, a new element has come into censorship disputes. It is said, for example, that the manner of presenting or advertising or distributing obscene or pornographic material is what constitutes the real offense because it intrudes on the privacy of others. This is the so-called "pandering" or "thrusting" argument. The emergence of the argument has an interesting background. In the *Stanley* case (1969) the Supreme Court held that neither a state nor the federal government can constitutionally punish mere possession of obscene material. (Of course, if one has the constitutional right to keep obscene material in private possession, it would seem logical to assume that he has the right to go out and purchase it on the open market. But the argument has not been carried this far.)

In the same year a three-judge federal district court in Massachusetts (*Karalexis* v. *Byrne*) held that, without prior evidence of pandering, admission of minors, or forced display to an unwilling public, motion picture theatres might be allowed to show to willing adult patrons what might otherwise be obscene movies.

More recently, the Supreme Court has upheld the constitutionality of a 1967 act of Congress which makes it possible for a homeowner to prevent a *second* mailing to his home of material that he does not care to receive. In effect what these decisions suggest is that the Court is trying to extricate itself from the necessity of ruling on censorship cases; that is, it is trying to put a lid on the Pandora's box it opened with its decision in the *Roth* case. The right *not* to receive, in other words, is coming to be regarded as the obverse of the right to own and possess. This, in effect, narrows the scope of censorship to the "pandering" or "thrusting" aspect.

In a recent statement the ACLU has said that the right of privacy means that a person cannot be compelled to be exposed to obscene material by having it thrust upon him against his wishes in public places where he cannot avoid it. For example, on a busy highway a huge billboard carrying a vividly suggestive movie ad might be an example of this kind of thrusting. The ACLU believes that a carefully and narrowly drawn statute prohibiting such thrusting would be constitutional (Statement May 11, 1970). But, if so, it would be upheld because it protects the right of privacy, not as a form of permissible censorship. Even so, one may have reservations about the thrusting argument. For example, a garish marquee sign may serve to *warn* the public against a particular film or to alert gullible movie-goers to the character of a particular film. So the argument against thrusting seems, in the end, to be self-defeating.

Censors tend to be humorless and unimaginative and to have little confidence in self-correcting processes. If, without censorship, motion picture producers bring out nothing but shockers and trashy sexies, a natural reaction is certain to set in over a period of time. Boredom is one of the most powerful social forces. The fact that Producer

A has made a fortune on a particularly offensive movie may induce others to make the same kind of film; that is, for a time, while it is profitable. But action breeds reaction, and sooner or later people will tire of seeing this kind of film. Sex themes have certain inherent limitations. There are only a limited number of ways of performing the sex act, and copulation is much more exciting to the parties than to an audience. Producers can play games with audiences by making one film a bit more daring than another. But sooner or later they come up against the tough question: "What do you do for a second act?"

I will not go so far as to paraphrase what Ronald Reagan once said about redwood trees by saying that once you have seen one nude, you have seen them all. Fortunately, this is not true. But it is quite obvious that once human beings have had too large a diet of anything, they tend to look for something else. Once all the old taboos have been broken, the disposition to break them necessarily abates. So, too, the shock value of such terms as *bullshit* or *mother fucker* rapidly abates. Whatever excitation hard-core pornography may possess can be dissipated by endless repetition. Controlled experiments conducted by Dr. Clifford B. Riefler of the University of North Carolina and his colleagues have demonstrated that a stag film may arouse the average young college man for one or two performances but soon becomes a bore. On the other hand, the lure of the forbidden is proverbial.

Denmark, which has always had a rather relaxed attitude to so-called obscene materials, recently decided to lift all legal bars to the production and sale of hard-core pornography to anyone over six years old. (Note: the exception is really ridiculous, for the 1-to-6-year-olds are not likely to exhibit much of an interest in such materials.) Lifting the bars had, of course, the immediate effect of stimulating sales because non-citizens flocked into Denmark out of curiosity, to have a look 'round and make a few purchases. While it is too early to draw any solid conclusions about the operation of the new law, still the fact is that the number of rapes has remained steady since it was adopted, but minor sex crimes have diminished by about 50 percent. (See "Denmark's Garden of Sex" by John Greton, *New Society,* October 30, 1969.)

Accepting their arguments at face value, censors have a better remedy at hand than enactment of statutes making the sale of obscene materials or the exhibition of obscene movies a criminal offense. They can peacefully picket bookstores and movies that have given offense. Recently, a group of young evangelists from San Francisco picketed a bookstore on New York's 42nd Street specializing in the sale of erotic materials. The evangelists carried signs reading: "Jesus is the Right Groove" and "Smut's a Rut." (*New York Times,* June 1, 1970.) True, the picket lines may have advertised the shop and stimulated sales, but that is a risk any protest runs.

If parents are alarmed about the danger of obscene materials, let them show more interest in their children, in what they read, in their leisure-time activities, in the quality of entertainment available to them. What is wrong with relying on parents, teachers, and clergymen to express *their* concern, without recourse to the criminal law? Booksellers and film makers and theatre owners are not immune to public pressure. Public pressure, unaided by any penal statutes, has eliminated objectionable racial and ethnic stereotypes from motion pictures, radio and television. Protests by Blacks, Mexican-Americans, Jews and other groups have been highly effective without the aid of criminal statues. Even more effective, in my view, would be sharp criticism by all the media critics of trashy publications and cheap movies. If the critics would zero in on some of the more objectionable of these *Valley-of-the-Doll* productions, there would be fewer of them.

But formal censorship is counter-productive as a practical remedy; and it is dangerous, for it will lead to other forms of censorship and repression. In a democratic society, criticism and popular concern are the best correctives. They are legitimate remedies; censorship is not. Censorship is for the Colonels in Greece.

But my rejection of censorship in all its forms cuts much deeper than these practical arguments suggest. Censorship is not what it appears to be. If we took censors at face value, we would believe that they are genuinely concerned about the harmful effect certain materials may have on others, principally but not exclusively on minors and also on disturbed adults, and on society at large. But censors do not understand their own motivations. For the most part, they are motivated by fear.

To a degree, fear that certain materials may have harmful effects on others and on society is genuine; but the real fear stems from a fear that the censor has about himself, about his own impulses and desires. If looking at nude photographs bothers him, he feels that it must have the same effect on others. And since he does not like to be bothered in this way—since he distrusts his own impulses—he feels that others must be protected, as he would protect himself. Basically this is why it is impossible to agree upon a legal definition of obscenity. Obscenity is a state of mind. In brief, the censor is the problem—not the qualities, whatever they may be, of the thing that he would censure.

In his history of literary censorship in England, Donald Thompson writes:

> *Political censorship is necessarily based on fear of what will happen if those whose work is censored get their way, or if they are effective in persuading a large number of readers to share their point of view. The nature of political censorship at any given time depends on the censor's answer to the simple question, 'What are you afraid of?'* (A LONG TIME BURNING: THE HISTORY OF LITERARY CENSORSHIP IN ENGLAND.)

The same question can be asked of those who would censure obscene materials. What is it that they are afraid of? There is no appeasing the fearful. "Fear," as Wordsworth wrote, "hath a hundred eyes that all agree/ To plague her beating heart." What is feared and censored at one time, may not be feared and censored at another. The dominant fears may shift from one generation to the next, and from place to place. In one period it may be that subversive materials must be kept from the susceptible out of a fear of unwanted social change. Or it may be that anti-Semitic or anti-Catholic propaganda must be banned out of the assumed need to protect Jews or Catholics. In a word, censorship—or the impulse to censure—is a constant in any society in which there are people who have unmanageable fears.

Today there is a special reason to be concerned about censorship because there are many reasons for people to be fearful. Most people today share a sense of profound historical dislocation. The pace of social and scientific and technological change generates this sense of dislocation, of social disruption, of social and institutional instability. In such a setting, Dr. Robert Jay Lifton notes, one impulse in response to confusion is to "simplify, clarify and suppress" (*The Nation,* June 29, 1970); above all, suppress, censor, stamp out. Whatever the individual motives of the censors may be, censorship is a form of social control. It is a means of holding a society together, of arresting the flux which the censors fear. And since the fear cannot be appeased, the demands for censorship mount in volume and intensity. And one form of censorship can easily lead to other forms.

Consider for example, the recent Supreme Court decision (May 7, 1970) upholding the constitutionality of a 1967 act of Congress to the effect that a homeowner can insist that there be no second mailing from anyone who sends material which postal patrons consider "erotically arousing and sexually provocative." The Supreme Court upheld this provision in broad and sweeping terms. The decision, ironically, was written by Chief Justice Burger who, we had been told, was a strict constructionist. It would take only minor amendments to this act to extend its provisions to include political material or social appeals or campaign material. Yet it had been assumed, prior to this decision, that citizens must put up with a certain amount of annoyance and affront, in the distribution of printed materials, as a minor price to pay for the values implicit in the First Amendment's guarantee of a free press. By such means is censorship extended from this to that, from what is sexually provocative to what is politically or sociologically or religiously provocative. Even business materials and sales promotions are not immune. *Advertising Age* (May 11, 1970) was quick to note that the Court's decision posed not merely a threat to the direct mail industry, but had "vast implications for advertising," as indeed it does.

And the dynamics of censorship—of the impulse to suppress—are such that if one form of censorship fails, other and more dangerous forms will be tried. For example, the underground press irritates and offends many highly proper persons by its language and its addiction to nude photographs, not to mention its politics. But since it is difficult to suppress a paper by constitutional means, "informal" means have been used, that is, censorship by harassment (see the article by that title, written by

Kingsley Widmer, in *The Nation,* March 30, 1970). In this article Mr. Widmer narrates the trials and tribulations of one underground paper in San Diego. "When the more formal restrictions slacken," writes Mr. Widmer, "authoritarian control finds other means." Illegal police harassment can constitute an effective form of censorship. And there are many other forms that censorship may take. Vice-President Agnew's strictures against the mass media have succeeded, to some extent at least, in forcing the media to be more cautious and circumspect and to give more space and attention to the Administration, and to present the Administration in a more favorable light than they had done before his attacks began. His speeches have carried a clear threat of possible government intervention, a threat which is most disturbing, of course, to the governmentally licensed electronic media.

Of all forms of censorship, self-censorship is perhaps the most effective; and fear—including the fear of formal censorship—stimulates self-censorship. No one can afford to overlook the fact that the various law and order proposals pending in the Congress, and the various measures proposed to curb crime, are part and parcel of a larger package which includes dozens of bills to cope with obscenity and the like.

But there is another dimension to the censorship problem. Historically, moral indignation, from which the impulse to censure springs, is much more recent than we imagine. Moral indignation has been defined as the disinterested tendency to inflict punishment. If A has been assaulted by B, A quite naturally wants to see B punished. This sentiment is as ancient as Cain and Abel. But if A has not been injured or damaged but, nevertheless, wants to see B punished for something that offends A's sense of social morality, then this constitutes a disinterested tendency to seek punishment. The sentiment of moral indignation has always been especially strong in the lower middle class; it scarcely exists in societies in which this class is of slight importance.

And it has not always existed; scholars have failed to isolate any sentiment in the ancient world that might fairly be characterized as moral indignation. Anger, wrath, screams of protests, demands for vengeance—yes; but moral indignation is another matter. Moral indignation is a resentment caused by the suppression of instinct. The lower middle class has learned (perhaps one should say "has been disciplined") to be frugal, to be abstemious, to work hard, to be sexually prudent, to save for a rainy day, etc. These restraints are part of the price it has paid for its precarious social position. Call these restrictions the Puritan Ethic or what you will, adherence to them generates the sentiment of moral indignation or resentment. The lower middle class does not like to discipline itself in these ways, and it resents those who reject such discipline or find it unnecessary. Resentment emerges as a secret, unconscious, unfocused tension felt in members of a group who vaguely sense their inferior social position, their lack of power, and whose rage is contained by transforming self-denial into a virtue (see comments by Dr. Matthew F. Dumont, *Science,* January

10, 1969).

The classic study of moral indignation is that by Dr. Svend Ranulf, published in this country by Shocken Books in 1964: *Moral Indignation and Middle Class Psychology*. Invariably, the lower middle class feels that it is *more* virtuous than the upper middle class which does not need to mortify its senses or curb its manner of living in order to scrape together enough money to pay the month's rent or the insurance premium. It is interesting to note that the class *below* the lower middle class is seldom inclined to be moralistic and self-righteous. Once a lower middle class family or individual begins to rise in economic and social status, the feeling of resentment, of generalized anger, tends to abate or, as Ranulf puts it: "the disinterested tendency to inflict punishment will tend to disappear when its bearers in the lower middle class grow rich."

Censors are infused with the sentiment of moral indignation—a dangerous and misleading sentiment because, by blinding those who voice it to the real reasons for their indignation, it makes them puppets whose fears can be manipulated for ends and purposes they do not foresee or intend. Often an upper-class group will appear to join in and encourage a censorship campaign because such campaigns are one of the ways of manipulating the lower middle class.

Dr. Alex Comfort has said that "the obscene is that which disturbs the sexually insecure." By and large, it is the lower middle class, and sections of the middle class, which are most deeply concerned with sexuality which is

deemed abnormal or which stimulates strong guilt feelings or intense curiosity which it might be dangerous to
gratify. Censorship is an attempt to suppress these fears.

But in a time of turmoil and rapid social change,
fears of this sort can become fused with other kinds of
fears; and their censorship becomes merely one aspect of
a general repression. The extent of the demands for censorship may be taken, therefore, as an indicator of the
social health of a society. It is not the presence—nor the
prevalence—of obscene materials that needs to be feared
so much as it is the growing demand for censorship and
repression. Censorship—not obscenity nor pornography
—is the real problem.

In 1969, Charles Keating was appointed by President Nixon to fill a vacancy in the Federal Commission on Obscenity and Pornography. Taking sharp issue with the findings of the majority, Mr. Keating submitted a minority report which was widely applauded among groups and magazines whose viewpoints he represents.

Mr. Keating was the founder in 1956 of the Citizens for Decent Literature, Inc., a non-profit, non-sectarian, non-political corporation with national headquarters in Cincinnati, Ohio, an organization dedicated to eliminate obscene literature. He is now legal counsel for that organization.

Mr. Keating has submitted amicus curiae *briefs in support of the prosecution in many important obscenity cases, including interventions to the U. S. Supreme Court in the famous* GINZBURG, MISHKIN, *and* FANNY HILL *cases.*

Charles H Keating, Jr.

THE VERY WORD *censorship* conjures up visions of book-burning, blue pencils, restricted shelves in libraries and puritanical boards gleefully consigning volumes to the flames. Despite this horrendous image, I think it is important we realize what censorship really involves. I think it is important we realize the need for laws against obscenity, laws designed to protect the public morality.

In a free country, does the government have a right to tell an adult what he can or cannot read? This question is often raised by well-meaning and intelligent people who are sincerely concerned about a possible loss of First Amendment freedoms.

The answer must relate back to the reason for the existence of obscenity laws. Obscenity laws exist because society recognizes that the distribution of obscenity is harmful to the *public* morality. Therefore, *for the greater good of the community at large,* obscenity laws were first enacted in England and eventually brought to this country by our founding fathers.

The constitutionality of obscenity laws was never specifically challenged until the Roth-Alberts case came up in 1957. In that case the U. S. Supreme Court, the official interpreter of the Constitution, said:

> *The unconditional phrasing of the Amendment was not intended to protect*

*every utterance . . . All ideas . . . having
even the slightest redeeming social importance have the full protection of the
guarantee . . . but implicit in the First
Amendment is the rejection of obscenity
as utterly without redeeming social importance. This rejection for that reason is
mirrored in the universal judgment that
obscenity should be restrained, reflected in
the international agreement of all 48
states, and in the 20 obscenity laws enacted by the Congress from 1842 to 1956.
This is the same judgment expressed by
this Court in* CHAPLINSKY V. NEW HAMP-
SHIRE . . . *'There are certain well-defined
and narrowly limited classes of speech, the
prevention and punishment of which have
never been thought to raise any Constitutional problem. These include the lewd
and obscene . . . such utterances . . . are of
such slight social value as a step to truth
that any benefit that may be derived from
them is clearly outweighed by the social
interest in order and morality . . .' We
hold that obscenity is not within the area
of constitutionally protected speech or
press . . . The test (is): whether to the
average person, applying contemporary
community standards, the dominant theme
of the material taken as a whole appeals
to the prurient interest.*

Despite inconsistencies in several cases ruled on by the Supreme Court since 1957, the Court has never changed the basic premise that obscenity is not constitutionally protected.

While upholding the constitutionality of obscenity legislation, the Court has been careful to build safeguards into the law that do assure protection of First Amendment freedoms. For example, the Court has held that "prior restraint" type censorship is clearly unconstitutional. For an official agency such as a censor board, postal authority, or other government agency to say that certain specific material cannot be printed, published, or sent through the mail is "prior restraint" and is clearly unconstitutional. The law says—and I agree—that one must be free to print, publish, or distribute *anything*—but that having done so, the individual is subject to laws he has violated. If you print and distribute libelous material, you are subject to prosecution under the libel laws. If you print and publish obscenity, you are subject to prosecution under obscenity laws. So, you see, we are dealing with a question of law enforcement and not a question of censorship.

To further protect First Amendment freedoms, the Court defined the word "obscene" to include the phrase "taken as a *whole* appeals to the prurient interest." It is a fact that prior to the 1957 Roth-Alberts case, attempts had been made to proscribe works of recognized literary value. The phrase "taken as a whole" requires that the complete work be considered, and not just any paragraph taken out of context. Thus, works that can be defended on the basis of artistic or literary value are afforded complete protection of the law.

There is widespread misunderstanding today to the effect that only material that is "utterly without redeeming social importance" can be proscribed. If you will refer back to the quotation from the Roth-Alberts decision, you will see that the Court said flatly that obscenity *is* utterly without redeeming social value, and did not include that phrase in the definition of the word "obscene."

Since the Roth-Alberts case, which was decided by a 7-2 majority, there have been many decisions in which a majority of the court voted to reverse convictions under obscenity laws; but the justices who made up the majority of the court at the time based their votes on differing reasons. "No-clear-majority" decisions such as those do not change basic law.

In 1966 the Court reversed the *Fanny Hill v. Attorney General of the State of Mass.* case. Three Justices—Fortas, Warren and Brennan—held that proscribed material must be "utterly without redeeming social importance." This view has never been held by a majority of the court and thus has never become a rule of law. If it ever does become the law, it will be impossible to proscribe anything, no matter how obscene. For *utterly* is an all-inclusive word. There are those who will say that if you can burn a book and warm your hands from the fire, the book has some redeeming social value. Certainly the law never intended that the most obscene work imaginable could be "redeemed" by including passages referring to the American flag, or apple pie, or motherhood.

While it is true that obscenity laws do restrict the freedom of the individual, it is equally true that many laws restrict individual freedom. It is by such restrictions that we preserve an orderly society.

*   *   *   *

Why a Presidential Commission?

> *The Congress finds that the traffic in obscenity and pornography is a matter of national concern.*

This opening statement of Public Law 90-100, creating the Commission on Obscenity and Pornography, is ample evidence that our nation is imperiled by an all-pervasive poison.

Pornography is not new. However, for centuries its invidious effect upon individuals and upon nations has been held in reasonable control through the operation of law.

It is apparent that the laws prohibiting obscenity and pornography have played an important role in the creativity and excellence of our society. It seems incredible to me that the majority of the Presidential Commission appointed under Public Law 90-100 has opted for a "Danish" solution to the problem of pornography: namely, to remove the controls, to repeal the laws.

The dictionary defines pornography as "originally a description of prostitutes and their trade." Pornography is not merely associated in this historical sense with prostitution; it is actually a form of prostitution because it advertises "sex for sale," offers pleasure for a price.

Sexual powers are intimately bound up with love and life—not merely with a momentary satisfaction of desire. Only a human being is capable of love; the lower forms of animal life experience pleasure as a mere sense reaction. A person is much more than a physical body. Any form of sexual activity which is impersonal, which uses the body solely for pleasure, violates the integrity of the person and reduces him to the level of an irresponsible animal.

The traditional Judeo-Christian ethic does not condemn pleasure as an evil; but it does condemn pleasure when its pursuit deliberately excludes higher purposes and values. Everybody knows that the appetite for food renders the necessity of eating more palatable, more pleasurable. To eat in order to live is rational; to live in order to eat is an abuse. The same is true of the sex drive. This drive serves both the individual and the common good of the human race when it ministers to love and life. Love is always fruitful of lasting good; mere pleasure is, of its nature, transitory and barren; the only residue is likely to be unhappy and remorseful memories.

Those who speak in defense of sexual morality are accused of making sex dirty. It's the other way around. The defenders of pornography are guilty of degrading sex. Marcel Proust, the famous French novelist, described the effect on himself of his early reading of erotica: "Oh stream of hell that undermined my adolescence." Literature reflects life more truly than does scientific opinion.

No, the state cannot legislate virtue, cannot create moral goodness by merely enacting law; but the state can and should legislate against vices which publicly jeopardize the virtue of people who prefer to remain virtuous. It is the proper function of law to offer citizens such protection.

The shocking and anarchistic recommendations of the majority of the Presidential Commission are difficult to comprehend. To advocate repeal of Federal laws and State statutes—in spite of the lessons of history, in spite of the will of the overwhelming majority of the people of this nation, and in spite of the circumstances of our times—is an advocacy of moral anarchy and a defiance of the mandate of the Congress which created the Commission!

Staying with the mandate of Congress in Public Law 90-100 which established the Commission, we find emphasized, by placement in Section 1 of that Act, the following statement:

> *The State and local governments have an equal responsibility in the exercise of their regulatory powers, and any attempts to control this transmission (i.e., of obscenity and pornography) should be a coordinated effort at the various governmental levels.*

It has long been apparent that not only are the States concerned but they have been responsible "in the exercise of their regulatory powers and attempts to control the transmission of obscenity and pornography." The police officer, the prosecutor, the District Attorney, and the Attorney General have not been remiss in vigorous enforcement of the law against the criminal pornographers; but they have been rebuffed and made ridiculous by the courts' subservience to the "no-clear-majority" decision of the Douglas-Black dominated (i.e., in the obscenity field) United States Supreme Court. Since 1967, insofar as obscenity cases are concerned, the forcing of immorality on the States by the United States Supreme Court has gone on unabated. Recent appointments, however, give hopeful indications that this disgusting erosion of morality may be checked. The sole legislative recommendation I made to the Administration and to the Congress was to return to the States the final *determination of fact* in obscenity cases, and not to permit a State's decision to be subject to appeal on the Federal level.

*   *   *

Some recommend that the law maintain a double standard; that is, that a certain level of obscenity would be deemed illegal for juveniles, and another level illegal for adults. Much pending State and Federal legislation is of this type. Such laws would make it a crime to sell or distribute obscenity to juveniles by means of incorporating into the law phrases such as "without redeeming value for juveniles" or "morally corruptive matter to juveniles," etc.

Certainly all right-thinking adults are concerned about keeping pornography out of the hands of juveniles. However, there is conclusive proof that this approach doesn't work. California and New York have both recently enacted legislation aimed at sales of obscenity to juveniles.

The New York law incorporates the "variable obscenity" concept: the law provides that the material be considered in relation to the audience at which it is aimed. It was under this concept that the U. S. Supreme Court upheld the conviction of Sam Ginsberg for selling to a juvenile girlie magazines that he could have sold legally to an adult. California set up an entirely separate section of the Penal Code aimed specifically at sales to juveniles, while retaining the section of the law aimed at sales to adults.

It is most obvious that New York and California have not solved their obscenity problem. In no other States will you see more pornography or more flagrant displays of pornography. There are several reasons for this.

First of all, the emphasis in the law on juvenile protection has lulled the citizenry into a kind of complacent acceptance of pornography in the community, aimed at the adult market. This complacency has made it much more difficult to organize an effective community campaign against obscenity.

Even more convincing are the following arguments against obscenity laws aimed at juveniles:

1. The emphasis on juvenile protection protects the producers of obscenity. By merely labeling their material "For Adults Only," they are free to supply hundreds of "adults only" outlets and place the major burden of law enforcement at the retail level rather than at the relatively few production sources.

2. The concept of juvenile protection has encouraged "adults only" smut shops to open in residential shopping areas. These outlets sell nothing but pornography: paperback books, picture magazines, still pictures, motion pictures, etc., and even display artificial sexual devices of every imaginable variety. Thus, under the guise of juvenile protection, the most perverse obscenity has moved from the back alleys of society into legitimate outlets. (A recent survey among teenagers by a Madison Avenue advertising firm asked "What sales slogan most attracts your attention?" The one mentioned most frequently was "Adults Only.")

3. Despite common misconceptions to the contrary, sales of obscenity to juveniles have never been a major problem. The emotional argument that portrays the pornographer as an ogre preying on children is just that—an emotional argument, not

fact. The commercial pornographer aims his product at adults. Juvenile names appear occasionally on the mail-order lists of pornographers, but that occurs by accident and not by design. Thus, laws aimed at protecting juveniles from obscenity miss the target completely and actually play right into the hands of the pornographer by, in effect, legalizing obscenity for adults. Once obscenity is allowed to exist legally in the community, much of it will end up in the hands of young people. They obtain it in many ways: from their father's dresser drawer, from newspaper drives conducted by the Boy Scouts, from the pervert who purposely disposes of his pornography near school grounds. *It is impossible to protect juveniles from pornography as long as it is legal for any segment of society to obtain it.*

4. Laws making sales of pornography to juveniles a crime are practically unenforceable. To my knowledge there has not been one case filed in California under the juvenile statute that was widely heralded as a solution to the problem. One reason is that, in fact, very few sales are made to juveniles. Another reason is the understandable reluctance of parents to involve their child as a prosecution witness in an obscenity case. Law enforcement personnel and postal inspectors will confirm that it is virtually impossible to set up such a case.

5. The double standard implicit in so-called "juve-

nile" legislation can only magnify the ever-widening generation gap. For adults to say, in effect: "It is O. K. for us to read dirty books, view dirty films, and receive dirty mail—but not for you kids" is a phony double standard. If material is obscene by the test of the law, it must be deemed obscene—period! If not, we create more problems than we solve.

*   *   *

Only one country in all modern civilization—Denmark—has attempted the drastic solution of legalizing obscenity for adults, while maintaining laws restricting sales or distribution of obscenity to minors. There are those in America, including the Presidential Commission majority, who would recommend the Danish approach as a solution to our pornography problem.

The advocates of this position point to Denmark as an enlightened society that has recognized the futility of attempting to legislate the morality of its people. Many articles about Denmark have been published in recent months, in America and in other countries, that contain wild distortions of the true state of affairs in that country.

For example, it is claimed that since pornography is no longer forbidden fruit in Denmark, everyone has lost interest in it and sales have actually dropped off. Therefore, that's the solution to the obscenity problem: legalize pornography and the problem will go away all by itself. Other recent articles about Denmark indicate that not only is pornography not bad—it is actually good: it protects society from the sex deviate who might otherwise commit anti-social acts. He now gets his kicks from legalized dirty books. To substantiate this theory, they point to a 31% statistical decrease in sex crimes in Copenhagen since obscenity has been legalized for adults.

But what is the true situation in Denmark? First of all, the only drop-off in pornography sales has been in the category of printed pornography—primarily paperback books. When pictorial pornography depicting every imaginable sexual deviation became legally available, no one would purchase the non-illustrated material; and those books became a drag on the market. Actually, there has been a tremendous increase in competition in Denmark since pornography has been legalized; and there is a great over-supply—not a lack of demand. This over-supply is being legally exported by Denmark—and illegally imported by other nations of the world. Production of pornography in Denmark is already estimated to be a one-hundred-million-dollar industry—three-quarters of which is exported. Thus, Denmark is now contributing to criminal activity on an international scale.

At my request Raymond P. Gauer, National Director of Citizens for Decent Literature, made a fact-finding trip to Copenhagen in January of 1970. Even in January, the worst time of year for tourists—there was then no sex-fair in progress—the porno shops that have proliferated in the city were crowded with Danes purchasing books printed in Denmark—in Danish. Even the respectable tobacco shops and news kiosks, on street corners and in hotels, carried hard-core pictorial pornography. The blatant facades of the porno or sex shops displayed large signs indicating they were open until 3:00 a.m. Many had conveniently placed vending machines on the sidewalks where one could purchase hard-core pornography, day or night, for a coin.

The number one circulation newspaper of Copenhagen, *Ekstra Bladet*, is a sex sheet from page one on. It publishes illustrations and photos that go far beyond the underground press of this country in sexual explicitness. Another large circulation newspaper, *BT*, is almost as bad. In the back of these newspapers there appear the sexually oriented personal ads, as well as large advertisements for live sex shows that are now legally conducted. These shows feature lesbian acts, male homosexuals, women and animals, as well as heterosexual activity of every imaginable variety—oral, anal, and vaginal. The shows include audience participation: men in the audience are invited on stage to be masturbated by nude female performers.

In the short time since pornography has been legalized in Denmark, the commercial exploitation of sex has led to almost complete degradation of that country, as pornographers compete to satisfy the demand for perversity that has been created. In January of this year, new picture magazines featuring sexual activity between women and animals had just come on the market, and were being touted by the porno shop operators. Other new material deals more and more with perversion: sadism, masochism, etc. Much of the new pornography is anti-religious, depicting monks and nuns in the most perverted types of sexual activity.

While it is supposedly a crime in Denmark to openly display pornography in shop windows, competition has caused many shopkeepers to flagrantly violate the law in order to attract customers into their stores.

An interview with Chief Deputy of Police Closter Christiansen indicated a deep personal concern on his part. He is concerned about raising his family in the moral climate that currently exists in Copenhagen. He pointed out that the 31% statistical decrease in sex crimes is misleading; violent sex crimes of forcible rape and assault have *not* decreased. The reason for the statistical decrease is that what had previously been a sex crime is now either legal or ignored. For example, the sale of pornography had been a sex crime. It is now legal. Laws against voyeurism have become impossible to enforce. Laws against rape are not enforced as long as the girl, regardless of her age, was a willing partner.

The FBI tells us that sex crimes in the United States are the most under-reported of all criminal activities— because of the embarassment of the parties involved. In a society like Copenhagen, where premarital sex and illegitimacy are socially accepted, where porno and sex shops display hard-core pornography throughout the city, where live sex shows are legally conducted, where the leading newspapers promote promiscuous sex on virtually every page—in such a society a girl would be ashamed to admit she had to be raped! It's a wonder that sex crimes in Denmark are reported at all!

In Denmark sex has been so badly commercialized and degraded that it is physically sickening. It is hard to imagine how that country can survive such permissiveness; surely it is much too early to fully assess the damage that has been done. Certainly, the citizens of this country will not tolerate the "Danish solution." What is rotten in Denmark would be positively putrid in America!

*   *   *

The Presidential Commission on Obscenity and Pornography based their recommended repeal of all Federal and State laws that "prohibit consensual distribution of sexual material to adults" on the statement that—

> *extensive empirical investigation, both by the Commission and by others, provides no evidence that exposure to or use of explicit sexual materials plays a significant role in the causation of social or individual harms such as crime, delinquency, sexual or nonsexual deviancy, or severe emotional disturbances.*

While a significant percentage of nationally recognized psychiatric authorities and many law enforcement officials at all levels of jurisdiction would disagree with that statement, the important point I want to make is that the reasons for obscenity laws are *not* contained in the statement. Historically, obscenity laws have existed in recognition of the need to protect the *public morality*.

The law, founded in reason and common sense, recognizes obscenity as intrinsically evil and does not demand the "clear and present danger" test so ardently advocated by civil libertarians. The law, rather, proscribes pornography on the basis of the public good—protecting public health and welfare, public decency, and morality, a condition absolutely essential to the well-being of the nation.

That obscenity corrupts lies within the common sense, the reason, and the logic of every man. If man is affected by his environment, by circumstances of his life, by reading, by instruction, by anything, he is then certainly affected by pornography.

I submit that never in the history of modern civilization have we seen more obvious evidence of a decline in public morality than we see today. The social statistics of venereal disease, illegitimacy, and the growing divorce rate reflect a promiscuous attitude toward sex which is doubtless formed of many factors—but certainly one factor has to be the deluge of pornography which screams at young people today.

To say that pornography has no effect is patently ridiculous. I submit that if pornography does *not* affect a person, that person has a problem. Pornography is intended to arouse the sexual appetite—one of the most volatile appetites of human nature. Once that appetite is aroused, it will seek satisfaction; and the satisfaction sought, without proper moral restraints, is often reflected in the social statistics discussed above.

The effects of obscenity on society can best be summed up by repeating here a quatrain written in 1705 by Alexander Pope:

> *Vice is a monster of so frightful mien,*
> *As to be hated, only needed to be seen.*
> *Yet seen too oft, familiar with her face,*
> *We first endure, then pity, then embrace.*

Those who recommend repeal of obscenity laws would have America embrace the monster vice.

At a time when the spread of pornography has reached epidemic proportions in our country and when the moral fiber of our nation seems to be rapidly unravelling, the desperate need is for enlightened and intelligent control of the poisons which threaten us—not the declaration of moral bankruptcy inherent in asking for the repeal of the laws which have been the defense of decent people.

To deny the need for control is literally to deny one's senses. Credit the American public with enough common sense to know that one who wallows in filth is going to get dirty. This is intuitive knowledge. Those who will spend millions of dollars to tell us otherwise must be malicious or misguided or both.

Any wholesale attempt to repeal obscenity statutes does not reflect the will of Congress, the opinion of law enforcement officials throughout our country, and worst of all, flouts the underlying convictions and desires of the great mass of the American people. Far from needing repeal of legislation controlling pornography, what is called for is a return to law enforcement. Law enforcement in the area of obscenity has been emasculated by the courts which are seemingly divorced from the realities of our communities. The courts determine from afar the standards of those communities.

The law is capable of coping with the problem of pornography and obscenity, but the law must be coupled with the logic that an American is innately capable of determining for himself his standards of public decency, and moreover, that he has a right to make that determination.

The words of Alexis de Toqueville (during his American visit, 1835-1840) seem appropriate:

> *I sought for the greatness and genius of America in her commodious harbors and ample rivers—and it was not there; in her fertile lands and boundless prairies—and it was not there. Not until I went to the churches of America and heard her pulpits aflame with righteousness did I understand the secret of her genius and power. America is great because she is good— and if America ceases to be good, America will cease to be great.*

After receiving a Master of Arts degree from the University of Minnesota in 1938 Eugene McCarthy was a teacher and professor for ten years. During World War II, he served in the War Department as technical assistant in military intelligence.

At the time of his election to Congress in 1948, he was acting head of the sociology department at the College of St. Thomas in St. Paul, Minnesota. He served as a member of the House of Representatives for 10 years.

After his election to the United States Senate in 1958, he served as a member of the Senate Committees on Finance and Government Operations, the Senate Select Committee on Standards and Conduct, and the Democratic Steering Committee. He recently concluded his second term.

Senator McCarthy is the author of six books, among which his most recent are THE YEAR OF THE PEOPLE *and* OTHER THINGS AND THE AARDVAARK.

Eugene McCarthy

THE PROBLEM OF CENSORSHIP raises three basic questions: first, what, if anything, should be censored? Second, assuming that some things should be censored, who is to do it and by what standards? And third is the practical question of whether any particular personal or social good results from censorship, even when there is agreement on the first two points.

One simple answer to the first question is that there should be absolute freedom of expression without any kind of restraint or limitation. This position is generally defended by the uncritical assertion that every person has the right to express his views or judgment on any subject, and the rather obvious limitations are usually demonstrated by irrelevant examples, such as denying a person the right to shout "fire" in a crowded theatre when there is no fire.

Theoretically, the only way to make public what is known, or thought known, is to have everyone talk or record everything he has thought for examination and judgment by others.

The real basis of freedom of speech and of expression is not, however, the right of a person to say what he thinks or what he wishes to say but the right and need of all persons to learn the truth. The only practical approach to this end is freedom of expression.

Although there have been periods in history in which there was little or no censorship, those periods have been more than offset by others in which efforts were made to control what was said, written, or otherwise communicated.

The earliest record of attempted censorship is of religious or political ideas. Generally in those times during which there was repression, or attempted repression, of religious or political ideas, there was little effort to control what today is called pornography or obscenity. Socrates was forced to take hemlock because of political ideas and political influence. There was, insofar as the record shows, no threat to Aristophanes because of the play *Lysistrata,* although nearly 2,400 years later Postmaster General Arthur Summerfield, in the Eisenhower administration, did rule that play was obscene and, therefore, could not be sent through the United States mails. He later reversed his order, not on the point of its being obscene or not, but by observing that he did not know the play was as old as it was. Evidently, he had different standards for old obscenity than he had for new or current obscenity. At the same time, the Post Office Department did not attempt to suppress the use of the mails to transmit within this country the *Communist Manifesto* or to take it out of libraries, nor were the publications of various atheistic societies denied the use of the mails.

Although there was continuous concern over religious heresy in the Middle Ages, Boccaccio did write his

Tales in the 14th century and published with a measure of freedom, as did Chaucer and others.

Since religious or political censorship is not being imposed in the United States today, nor is it being seriously advocated (and there is little likelihood that such advocacy will occur), the current problem of censorship relates principally to pornographic or obscene writings, pictures, and other representations or communication.

As soon as one raises this matter, the very difficult problem arises to determine what, in fact, is obscene or pornographic. Attempts have been made to distinguish between "hard-core" pornography and "borderline" pornography. The courts, in some cases, have tried to rule not on the substance of the material itself but on the intent of those who were producing it or attempting to dispense it, suggesting that if the purpose was to make money or profit, what was sold, therefore, became pornographic and subject to censorship. In some cases an attempt was made to make distinctions on the literary quality of the material. The principle seemed to be that if pornography was well done it could be disseminated, but if it was not well done it could be suppressed. This always seemed to me to be a very strange ruling, since one might assume that what was well done would be more effective and have more influence than that which was badly done or in poor taste.

The problem of distinction is very difficult. It has always been hard for traditional religions to separate clearly the obscene from the religious. "The Canticle of

Canticles" is accepted as a part of the Christian Bible. The Indian penal code exempts religious books and pictures from the anti-obscenity laws of the country. In somewhat the same way, when the humane slaughter bill was being considered by the Congress a few years ago, it was proposed that the standards should not apply to the killing of animals when such killing was done pursuant to certain religious ceremonies or according to religious prescriptions.

Although the question as to what is obscene or pornographic and subject to censorship has not been satisfactorily answered, we must, nonetheless, go on to the second question as to who is to decide what is to be censored. There is no institution nor any one person, with the exception of the Pope in the Catholic Church, who is given limited claims of infallibility, and who can with any absoluteness assert that this is the truth or that this is the truth's speaker.

There is no satisfactory answer to the question as to who should exercise censorship. In the United States a number of devices have been tried, none of which has been very satisfactory. For example, the motion picture industry developed a code and chose a person to act as a non-official censor. State legislatures have set up special committees on censorship to study the problem; and in some cases, state commissions have been set up to pass judgment on movies and other forms of communication. Purely advisory and non-official organizations, such as the Legion of Decency, have been established to make public their judgment on books, television programs, motion pictures, art exhibits, and the like. In some instances the final judgment is left to police commissioners and other civil authorities. Some cases have been carried through state courts and, ultimately, to the Supreme Court of the United States. In no case do we have certainty or clarity.

This brings us to the third question: namely, whether or not there is any evidence that censorship, or the lack of it, has had any significant effect upon society.

There is nothing in the historical record to show that censorship of religious or political ideas has had any lasting effect. Christianity flourished despite the efforts of the Roman Emperors to suppress it. Heresies and new religions developed and flourished in the Christian era at the height of religious suppression. The theories of democracy did not die out even though kings opposed them. And the efforts in recent times to suppress the Communist ideology and to keep it from people has not had a measurable or determinable success. Insofar as the record goes, the indications are that heresy and political ideas either flourished or died because of their own strength or weakness even though books were suppressed or burned and authors imprisoned, exiled, or executed.

The record is much less clear with reference to the effects of suppression of pornography or obscenity. The control or suppression of pornography, like all censorship, is based on belief in the power of an idea to move men to action.

The question is whether there is a connection between pornography and violent or anti-social behavior. This question is probably unanswerable one way or the other although the President's Commission on Pornography and Obscenity in a report just recently published states that "there is no evidence that exposure to pornography operates as a cause of misconduct in either youths or adults." The report was rejected by the Administration even before it was published. Undoubtedly, a new commission will be set up and its findings may contradict those of the first; and the second could be followed by a third which will continue to leave us in utter confusion.

Earl Finbar Murphy, in an article in the *Wayne Law Review* in 1964, cites two examples of violent behavior which show the real impossibility of coming to any clear conclusion about pornography as the cause of anti-social behavior. According to Murphy, Heinrich Pommerenke, a rapist and mass slayer of women in Germany, was supposedly moved to his actions by seeing Cecil B. DeMille's movie *The Ten Commandments*. The Jewish women dancing about the golden calf moved him to conclude, according to the report, that women were the source of all the world's trouble and that it was his mission to remove them by executing them. John Haigh, the British vampire, reportedly was incited to murder and to the method of the vampire as a result of watching Anglican High Church services.

The real case, and perhaps the only one, for censorship of pornographic material may be that made in an article in the *Washington Post* on September 13, 1970, by

Reo M. Christenson of the Department of Political Science at Miami University in Ohio. He argued for stronger pornography legislation on the grounds that, according to a Gallup Poll, three-fourths of the American people want such legislation. "They are affronted by books, magazines, movies, plays. . . ."

The attendance records set by films which are alleged to be pornographic, such as *I Am Curious—Yellow,* cast doubt on whether people are affronted by such films.

Official or legal censorship after the act may be a much less serious problem than the selection and control of information and ideas by those who do not produce the information itself.

Who determines who is to speak and write, since not everyone can speak?

Who selects what is to be recorded or transmitted to others, since not everything can be recorded?

There is danger in the concentration of control in the television and radio networks, especially in the large television and radio stations; danger in the concentration of ownership of the press, and in the relatively recent development of nationally syndicated columnists; danger in more or less standardized education for the entire country, and danger in the increasing concentration of selection by book publishers, and reviewers and by the producers of motion pictures and of radio and television programs.

The Government—particularly the Department of Defense—exercises great control over information. In the name of National security, the withholding of almost any item of information is justified; and even more affirmatively, not just the right to withhold information but to make false statements.

Withholding information from the Congress and from the public is now routine. This practice makes any effective congressional or public control of foreign policy or military policy almost impossible. The practice grew up in response to what were considered to be the demands of National security in wartime. But in peacetime, or in a state of less than total war, the practice has not diminished. In most cases the requirements of National security, although invoked, are not at the root of the matter. For example, during the past two years a subcommittee of the Senate Foreign Relations Committee, chaired by Senator Stuart Symington of Missouri, has been investigating United States defense commitments around the world. The subcommittee encountered great difficulty in obtaining information about our activities in, and our relations with, Laos, Thailand, the Republic of China, Japan, and Korea. The State and Defense Departments were unwilling to agree to the release of the transcripts of hearings that gave, for example, the details of funds paid to governments to induce them to send their troops to fight in Vietnam. The executive branch insisted on deletion of material from the transcript which although it would not damage the National security, would raise questions about the judgment of officers of the present administration and even of officers of previous administrations. The subcommittee staff commented:

> *The traditional reason for deletion—information the release of which would harm national security—has been expanded to include not only material which could be embarrassing to past or present foreign governments or their officials, but also to our government and its officials.*

In one case, that of the Philippines, the information they wished to keep secret had already been made public in the Philippines. Thus, apparently the American public and its elected representatives alone were to be kept in ignorance of the use to which American funds were put.

Another case which has become a classic example of misrepresentation is the Gulf of Tonkin affair. The incident, or incidents, in the Tonkin Gulf in August, 1964, was presented by the Johnson administration to the American people and to the Congress as a case of unprovoked attacks by North Vietnam on American warships on innocent patrol in international waters. In retaliation United States planes bombed North Vietnam, and at the President's request, the Congress passed the Tonkin Gulf resolution which came to be used as a blank check for escalating the Vietnam war. Over four years later, we learned that the events in the Tonkin Gulf were of a rather different character than we had been led to believe, that there may well have been provocation, and that retaliation by the United States was probably ordered before confirmation was received that the second attack had actually occurred.

The extent of American activities in Laos since the agreement of 1962, which theoretically neutralized that small, landlocked area next to Vietnam, was confirmed only in 1970 by the Symington subcommittee, although reports appeared in the press over the years. In June of 1970, AID Administrator John Hannah confirmed publicly that CIA agents use the civilian aid mission in Laos as a cover for their operations.

Insofar as the health of American democracy is concerned, this control over news and information by government and non-governmental powers is, in my opinion, much more dangerous than freedom of expression and publication.

After graduating from George Watson's Ladies' College in Edinburgh, Dame Rebecca West served as reviewer on the staff of FREEWOMAN *and as political writer for the* CLARION. *She has since contributed to many leading English and American newspapers as literary critic and political writer.*

Dame Rebecca West received her D.Litt. from New York University and was awarded the Chevalier of the Legion of Honour in 1957. She is a member of the American Academy of Arts and Sciences. She was awarded a C.B.E. (Commander of the British Empire) in 1949 and a D.B.E. (Dame of the British Empire) in 1959.

She has written numerous books since the publication of HENRY JAMES *in 1916. His most recent works are* A TRAIN OF POWDER, THE FOUNTAIN OVERFLOWS, THE COURT AND THE CASTLE, *and* THE VASSALL AFFAIR.

Rebecca West

THE IDEA OF CENSORSHIP is unworkable but not unthinkable. It cannot be denied (except by people so liberal as to be as insane as the wildest anti-liberals) that it is well within the bounds of possibility for certain information and opinions to be sufficiently dangerous to justify society in prosecuting anyone who publishes them. For example, if a book were issued consisting of arguments that the murder of unpleasant people should not be considered criminal, and recipes were presented for dispatching these undesirables by poisons hard to trace, society would have to do something about it. But even slightly removed from such forthrightness, the machinery of suppression becomes unworkable because it cannot be generally respected.

It is natural that society should wish to remove from its midst all activities which lead to corruption and disruption. Most spectacular among these are various manifestations of the sexual instinct. Prostitution spreads venereal disease, sets up its armies of pimps and blackmailers, and continually turns out into destitution its superannuated employees. Adultery can affect husbands and wives and children with various forms of material and psychological inconvenience. Sexual assault is obviously harmful. All these activities cause suffering to individuals and threaten the self-perpetuating aim of society, though to a degree and an extent often exaggerated by those afflicted by fear of sex.

It would seem obvious that a useful means of exterminating these anti-social factors would be the suppression by censorship of books, pictures, and public entertainments which stimulate the sexual instincts in a way likely to produce these activities. There is nothing inherently stupid in such a notion. Plato would have approved it; and we are not yet in a position to gainsay him.

But once a culture develops sufficiently to become sceptical, the idea of censorship becomes less attractive. To suppress a book or a picture or a sculpture or a play or a film is a terrible act of aggression against the artist who created it. This is a miming of capital punishment; it destroys the life that has been emanated by a life. Before such a step is taken, the majority of society should agree that the artist deserves such draconian punishment, or society will be suspected by its members of gross and heartless injustice. This would amount to a social threat which can, in certain circumstances, be as grave as any offered by sexual abuse.

Unfortunately, such majority agreement seldom comes into existence, because concepts of what is and what is not permissible in the sphere of sex differ from individual to individual, from class to class, from age-group to age-group, and from region to region. The only agreement likely to appear spontaneously and impressively occurs when a censured work is followed by an accusation that the censors were moved by a fear of innovation. Such an accusation is often true. The trouble is that it will, as likely as not, be the only accusation made with precision. All the other accusations will relate to opinions as to what is permissible or impermissible in the sexual sphere; and such opinions are often impossible to drag over the threshold of the unconscious into areas illuminated by logic.

Let me give an experience of mine which proved to me how much we work in the dark in relation to sex. When I was young, I read with some amazement several pages written by a scholar named Paul Elmer More who had everything that makes a great critic except taste. More laid a charge of excessive sensuousness against certain poets because their poetry contained frequent references to hair. Not pubic hair. Not even hair on the chest. Just hair where it is most publicly seen. On the head. And the head, for Mr. More, indicated heterosexuality; for he was criticizing male poets, and the heads discussed were female heads.

In an essay dealing with Yeats and Arthur Symons, he wrote:

> *There is one trick of both (though it is much more marked in Mr. Yeats) which may seem trivial, and yet does in some way connect itself with the total impression of their art. There is an insistence on the hair in describing women. Just why this habit should smack of decadence is not quite clear to me, but the feeling it inspires is unmistakable. Out of curiosity*

*I counted the number of allusions to hair
in the few poems that make up Mr. Yeats's*
WIND AMONG THE REEDS *and found they
mounted up to twenty-three.*

This observation struck me as strange, indeed. In certain circumstances I had been told that my hair was pretty, but this had always seemed to me among the less lecherous compliments I was paid.

The years passed; and I went the other day to stay with a friend much younger than myself, a middle-aged woman, who has a son of seventeen who attends a famous school nearby where students are allowed to dress as they like. He is a beautiful young man, and he looks magnificent with long and thick curling hair. He was talking about one of his school-fellows who, he said, had had a rough time at the rehearsal of a school play because the master, who was directing, had a prejudice against long hair, and this boy wore his hair down to his waist. He spoke with a fierce joy and with overtones of sexual and political revolt about his friend's hair, as if it were a banner of defiance which he had fortunately been able to grow instead of his friend. He said, contemptuously, "Of course, you can see what old Bugs (the master) was on about. He's getting bald himself."

He could not believe it when his mother and I said that we doubted whether the master was suffering from envy because he could not wear his hair down to his waist; and he was only partly convinced by the laughter that overcame us when we considered the possibility.

His mother and I were able to tell him honestly that to us hair was simply hair; and though we had worn it short or long during our lives, it had meant nothing to us either way.

Later his father came in and assured his son that to him, too, hair was out of the emotional field. He had always worn his short, and it had never occurred to him till that moment that he could have grown it long, and this was neither here nor there. The revelation upset the boy. He looked at his father as if sorry to realize that he suffered from a handicap to be compared to deafness. It all seemed great nonsense, till I thought of Paul Elmer More. He and this boy were opposed, but both knew something that the three of us did not. Or the boy's father and mother and I knew something that the boy and Paul Elmer More did not. There is simply no way of finding out which view is correct.

I was to remember this conversation later, when there was a question of censoring *Hair* in an English provincial town. We have now no central censorship of plays in Great Britain, but local authorities have at their command various procedures by which a play cannot be performed within their locality. A member of one of these authorities publicly called on his colleagues to protect their neighborhood from a visit of the touring company of *Hair*.

Now, I had not been neutral about the performance of *Hair* I had seen in London. It had depressed me greatly because of its resemblance to the cabaret performances I used to see in Berlin and Hamburg just at the time the

Weimar Republic was going underground. There was nothing subjective in this impression, for I found that other people with memories had also been struck by the resemblance which extended even to the lighting.

But in a railway carriage I was brought back to another aspect of it. Two women who both lived in the town where it was sought to ban *Hair* were discussing it; and one, a woman of forty-five, was all for the ban, and the other, at least ten years the younger, was violently opposed to the ban. It turned out that neither had seen the play, and they were judging *Hair* solely by the title. The older woman said that that title was disgusting; it made her think of all those horrible young men who went out with filthy long hair and beards. The other woman protested that that was how the young men wanted it and they were right; they knew what they were doing; the world would be much better from now on; it was time we put an end to hypocrisy.

Again, I was back with Paul Elmer More and the schoolboy. No doubt these two women may have heard that some of the actors and actresses were nude, and that sexual intercourse and masturbation were simulated on the stage, but they felt they were expressing themselves adequately on the question of censorship by simply using the word *hair* as a counter.

I was greatly relieved when I learned that the local authority did not ban *Hair*. The harm *Hair* could have done to society was not as great as the harm that could have been done by silencing the persons responsible for the production, and preventing them from making that point which was visible to them and invisible to me. Banning would have aroused distrust of the authorities and of all social arrangement which operates through authority. If *Hair* can be performed wherever it is commercially feasible, then the spectators can exercise their right to go and see it or stay away; and no harm is done beyond the immediate impact of the performance.

But, nevertheless, there are areas in which society should think a long time before abandoning its power to censor. It is dangerous to publish books or exhibit pictures or allow plays to be staged which recommend the pursuit of pleasure through cruelty. And there is a subsection to this class which is so dangerous that, in my opinion, it should be prohibited altogether. When sadistic pornography alludes to adults only, this does not constitute a general danger. The power to damage depends on the number of psychotics in our midst. It is probable that the ladies depicted in kinky boots wielding whips do not wield them too fiercely when they are encountered in life. They and their pornographic images may simply be provoking a simple physiological reaction which people have a right to enjoy if they have such tastes. But when pornography concerns itself with children, it is straying into mined territory.

The attitude of society towards intercourse between adults and children is highly confused. The act inflicts terrible and lasting suffering on the participants who would themselves not have participated had they themselves not been confused. In that state of confusion they were precipitated into a state of outlawry. The children involved are treated with hot injustice. In some cases, they may be mercenary little monsters who exploit their attractiveness to inflame adults whom they tempt and then blackmail. But in many instances, the child is a victim of precocious sexuality, and experiences a desire for a pleasure which he feels can be shared with an adult. It would be unfair to presume that this desire need be gross or vicious. It may well be that a child who is sexually precocious and also intellectually and emotionally precocious, and indeed of outstanding quality, could achieve a relationship with an adult which would be tender and affectionate and rewarding for both partners.

But surely society is right in attempting to eliminate such relationships. It does not want girl children to have children. It does not want boys committed to homosexuality when that may not be their real nature. It knows very well that boys and girls must be inexperienced in the most difficult art of judging character, particularly when they are deluded by sexual desire. It knows that the desire for sexual intercourse with children is found among people of infantile sexuality who probably have only a physical use for their child partners; and it knows that a number of these individuals are psychotics who link the idea of sexual intercourse with the idea of murder.

It is also a great convenience in family and social life if adults and children can mix freely under the shelter of a convention that sexual relationships between them are impossible. It is more than a convenience, for it must be remembered that the mass of children are averse to such relationships. This is partly due to a desire to fall in with their elders' prejudices, but it is also a matter of taste. Many children find adults big, clumsy, unpredictable in response, and physically repellent, and it is natural that they should; and many children dislike all manifestations of sex as much as their sternest guardians would wish.

The logic of the situation is so strong, and the emotions involved so ignorant of logic, that it is no wonder that the common reaction to such a situation is simply explosive. Whatever element there is today that is releasing itself in violence is manifest in child assault. In Great Britain the murder rate has not risen significantly in late years; but if one looks to quality and not quantity, the prospect is alarming. We have in the last few years had some revolting sexual murders of children, of which the worst was the Moors Murder case, which was without precedent in callousness and nasty joy. But there was also a disconcerting change of attitude among those who were not criminals. They plainly felt a lively venom against the child involved in sexual matters.

This was shown by the popularity of Nabokov's *Lolita,* which enjoyed a success in what is called "light reading," in spite of the fact that the story concerns a school-girl who is dragged 'round the country against her will, and who is at the mercy of a man who inflicts on her sexual intercourse of a kind which causes intense pain. If this kind of tale produces relaxation in the reader, life is even odder than we thought, and there might be another interpretation of its success.

In Nabokov's *Ada,* the little girl who is sexually involved (not with an adult, with a boy of fourteen, but their sexuality is adult enough from a physical point of view) is split into two. Ada represents the little-girl-lover as she is appreciated by her partner, a fresh and unspoiled embodiment of springtime; her sister Lucette represents the little-girl-lover as she is detested by her partner, an obscene monster who must be refused the indulgence she asks, and must be punished by total destruction. Lucette ends by going over the side of an Atlantic liner.

That the reading public is not revolted by the literary expressions of such attitudes, but takes them to their heart, is perhaps due to a revulsion against the worship of the child which has been a feature of Western life ever since Professor Freud's voice began to be heard outside Vienna, and evoked an answering call from the newly emergent class of pediatricians.

Psychoanalysts and spocks have worked together to make parents feel that their relationship to their offspring is the most important of all relationships, since the future of the race depends on that relationship. If baby does not have enough orange juice or suffers frustration then or later, humanity will be warped. This is true; but its application was faulty, as Freud and his daughter were eager to point out. Children need freedom to develop, but not more than they need discipline and responsibility. Otherwise, they come unprepared into adult life, and that, too, imperils the future.

Parents sank into a state when they accepted the dictum that every misfortune that befell their child, and any inadequacy that child showed, were entirely their parents' faults, and that a good parent ought to spend his life in expiation. An idol which demands too many burnt offerings becomes a bore; yet the faith which demands sacrifices is usually the longest to survive.

But behind closed doors, whether material or mental, there may be mutterings. Such discontent may account for the curious withdrawal of sympathy from a child who complains of sexual molestation by her elders. Such complaints, however justified, can make parents and teachers and even doctors treat the most blameless little liar, seeking to make herself interesting, as if there were something unclean about her; and that feeling may be strong enough to shadow her life.

Some years ago, in a village that I know, the local children were exposed to a frightening and painful experience at the hands of a farm laborer who had recently come to work in the district. He would waylay little boys and litle girls and flog them with nettles, and he would have an orgasm while he was assaulting them. The parents informed the police. After a hearing before magistrates, the man was committed for trial at the local assizes. The trial did not take place for five months; and during that period, I accidentally heard that the farm laborer had previously been employed by friends of mine in another district, and that he had left them because he had been arrested on a charge of child assault, and had been given a suspended sentence on condition he undergo psychiatric treatment. He had, in fact, concluded his treatment not very long before he arrived in this village where he had committed these new offenses. This information could not, of course, be given to the court till after the verdict had been reached. Lacking this evidence, the court behaved with a prejudice which was astonishing. The counsel, the jury, the spectators, all conveyed that they thought it probable that the children were little liars. The counsel for the defense shouted at the children when their evidence showed slight differences from their first statements—which was natural enough— and the judge did not protect the children. Even after the jury had reluctantly found the man guilty, and the court was informed of the farm laborer's previous conviction, there was no sense of urgency in the way he was treated. He was again put under an obligation to have psychiatric treatment. *But the children were treated with some reserve for quite a long time after.*

I do not wonder that society finds itself confused in such a situation. The situation itself is confused beyond clarification. I once served on a jury at our local assizes, and sat in court to listen while an earlier case was tried. A farm laborer of a high type, a skilled stockman, was charged with having incestuous relations with his little daughter. It was disclosed by the counsel for the prosecution and the counsel for the defense, acting in concert, that the man's wife had become insane two years prior, and he had been left to take care of his young family. This little girl of eleven, the eldest in the family, had been of great help to him. She was, they said, an exceptional child, old for her age, and very pretty and intelligent. About a year before, the man had made desperate attempts to get some local society to have the girl adopted.

He had implored them to take her away from his home; but the social workers, investigating the case, saw no reason why she should go. They had refused to move the child, and unwittingly had left the man alone with his temptation. Finally, neighbors realized what was going on, and the police stepped in. The court showed a civilized heart. The judge sentenced the man to nine-months imprisonment, but said he was doing this because he thought the convicted man was in need of time to rest and to be alone, and that social workers would see to the disposal of his child for the time being. The judge said he hoped that others would help the man sort out his troubles when he was in prison. But the man wept and wept; it was hard to think he would ever stop.

I was less remotely involved in yet another case. In a village where one of my relatives lives, a girl of fourteen suddenly told her parents that the very handsome young man who had recently bought a garage in the district had assaulted her under circumstances involving perversity and sadism. She repeated her story to her parents, to a schoolmistress, and to the widow of a past vicar of the parish, a magistrate who was mother confessor to the village. Her story did not vary, and though the vicar's widow advised caution, the parents resolved to call in the police. Fortunately, the mother was questioned by a neighbor who was a close friend, and who wanted to know why she looked so worried. When this friend heard the story, she told the mother on no account to go to the police; and she gave an excellent reason. She had a daughter who had gone to the same school as the girl who was making the complaint, and she had recently found in her daughter's chest-of-drawers, among her clothes, some mimeographed sheets which told exactly the same story about two fictional characters that the girl had been telling about herself and the garage proprietor. The friend and her husband had then ascertained that their daughter and her schoolfriends had found out that they could buy pornographic literature in mimeographed form at some of the market stalls in the nearest town; and they had put their pocket-money together to buy a few stories, among which was this particular tale. Had not that disclosure been made at the right time, the garage proprietor, who had a young wife and two little children, might have been ruined.

Even if the girl could not prove her story, her testimony would have raised suspicion between the garage-man and his wife. Moreover, the community would repeat that ancient lie about there being no smoke without fire. As it was, the girl was looked on by her own family as polluted and dangerous, and their relationship can never be the same again.

It must be assumed that the schoolgirl could not help telling lies about the garage proprietor. Till then, her family and her teachers had found her affectionate, truthful, and reliable. It must also be assumed that the adults surrounding her could not help reacting to her collapse with hostility instead of with sympathy. There had been a head-on collision between the girl's sexual instincts—strong with the strength of youth and wholly frustrated—and between the social instincts of her elders, which were based on experience. The decline of their own sexual instincts may also have been a factor. In any case, the persons concerned lost their real characters, and suffered the woes of partial schizophrenia.

Since sexual relations between adults and children lead to such suffering, surely it would be as well not to stimulate interest in this form of intercourse. For this reason there is a case for banning literature on this theme. I cannot believe in the theory that if people read pornography which deals with their own obsessions, whatever they may be, they will be content to enjoy these obsessions by reading about them and they will not seek to translate their fantasies into reality. If we find a man's home full of pictures of and books about sailing boats, and he lives by the sea, we will surely be wrong if we assume that he never gets into a boat. I am, therefore, all for censorship of books and pictures which deal with this particular manifestation of the sexual instinct; but I see little sense in applying censorship to a wider field. *De minimus lex non curat.*

That Latin tag is a good guideline for what to do with public entertainments where people appear naked or indulge in simulated sexual intercourse, and with books in which four-letter words describe the whole course of a sexual exploit, blow by blow. Such entertainments have existed since the beginning of time. Ever since there have been films, there have been "blue" films. There are none produced today which are any bluer than those produced by a famous director in early Hollywood. Whether these artifacts are banned or permitted is probably of slight importance.

As for the four-letter words, half the population has been using them without restraint from time immemorial. The only change in the scene is that now some of the other half of the population have joined in. One has to be something of a bonne bourgeoise to say *fuck* with assurance. Reading such words or printing them cannot be of much importance, and can be taken simply as a matter of taste. There is a sense that the use of four letters is part of a liberating movement that may translate into reality such long cherished ideals as universal peace, but it is not easy to see why. Millions of people were saying *fuck* when America went into Vietnam; and that the number may have slightly increased since then seems no reason for hoping that America will get out of Vietnam.

Ernest van den Haag is both a practicing psychoanalyst and a teaching professor of philosophy. At New York University he is Adjunct Professor of Social Philosophy, and at the New School for Social Research is a lecturer in both sociology and psychology.

Professor van den Haag studied at the Universities of Florence, Naples and the Sorbonne. He received his M.A. from the State University of Iowa and his Ph.D. from New York University.

The author of numerous articles and books, he recently achieved wide acclaim as author of THE JEWISH MYSTIQUE, *which has been widely reviewed.*

Ernest van den Haag

IN TIMES PAST, censorship[1] was intended to hinder the spread of philosophical and political ideas thought to undermine the social order—the institutions which shape the relations of men to each other. Such censorship of ideas continues in Communist and, to a lesser degree, in populist and in old-fashioned authoritarian societies; but in democracies it has been abandoned. There is insufficient agreement on what ideas to protect; more important, there is a widespread impression that one (or more) of the following propositions is correct and inconsistent with censorship.

1. In a free marketplace of ideas, the best ideas will win; without a free marketplace, they will not. (I know of no evidence for either proposition.)

2. There is no certain way to separate innocuous from noxious ideas; at least

[1] The distinction between "censorship" proper (advance governmental licensing of public communications) and the *post facto* prosecution of lewd publications although important is not relevant here. Censorship here refers primarily to governmental prohibitions, not to inability to publish because of rejections, *sua sponte,* by some or by all individual publishers, unless these rejections are centrally, monopolistically, and purposefully organized. Secondarily, "censorship" may refer to organized *pressures* on publishers to refrain from publishing what they might otherwise publish, but not to dissuasions.

public authorities are unlikely to seek or find one. (There is some evidence for the last proposition.)

3. Individuals have a right to form and communicate any belief. Society has no right to hinder them, or those who wish to read or see their material. (This is an axiom rather than a proposition and not subject to proof or disproof.)

4. A shared value belief system is not necessary for society. Or, perhaps, (a) freedom leads to such a system; or (b) freedom will not undermine it; or (c) censorship could not protect such a system anyway or; (d) censorship would cause damage in excess of any benefit. (This argument will be considered below.)

While some measure of freedom can be justified on other grounds, these propositions seem wrong to me in different degrees and for different reasons. Yet democratic societies have accepted them. Censorship has been abolished, with the exception—universal until quite recently—of sexual matters.

This exception is puzzling. What is to be achieved

by penalizing obscene communications?[2] What would be lost if they were permitted? It seems odd that, having abandoned the defense of the social and political order against subversive ideas, the censor should make a stand on what appears to be a comparatively trivial and semi-private cultural matter. Is censorship, then, a historical remnant? or could it be that obscenity threatens the social order in a more fundamental and pervasive, if less acute, way than political ideas do?[3]

Anti-obscenity statutes usually prohibit the sale of materials which appeal dominantly to the "prurient interest" of the purchaser.[4] Thus the laws seem to be directed against the sexual stimulation, for the sake of which the obscene materials are purchased. Yet it is unlikely that sexual stimulation in itself (or the sale of the means to it) can be regarded as wrong. We permit most other demands to be stimulated and satisfied by commercial means. Moreover, we do not prohibit sexual stimulation when the means themselves are not "ob-

---

[2] For the sake of brevity, all sexual materials—communications, pictures, spectacles, etc.—to be subjected to censorship are referred to as "obscene" or "pornographic." A distinction used to be made between *obscene* (dirty, and always disapproved) and *pornographic* (writing about whores or, more generally, writing invitingly about sex, and not always disapproved). Whatever distinctions may be useful require a different vocabulary now.

[3] I have to ignore the historical background of obscenity legislation.

[4] In the U. S., the materials must also violate "contemporary standards" and not be part of something that, as a whole, has "even the slightest redeeming social importance."

scene." Both sexes are openly invited to arouse their mutual desire by purchasing goods and services to that end; and much public entertainment is based on sexual allure, literary or pictorial. Even chemical means of stimulation—such as drugs promising to increase potency or desire—are quite legal. Why, then, is "obscene" stimulation not?

Censorship obviously is not opposed to the sale of psychic sexual stimulants in general. It must be addressed then to a specific *kind* of sexual incitement, to the means purveyed to produce it and, possibly, to a distinctive effect it is thought to have.

What kind of sexual stimulation does pornography provide? While dreary and repulsive to one part of the normal (most usual) personality, pornography is also seductive to another: it severs sex (the Id) from its human context (the Ego and the Superego) and thus from reality, from morality, from restraints, from sublimations and indeed all but the most archaic and infantile emotions. Pornography reduces the world to orifices and organs, human action to their combinations. Sex rages in an empty world; people use each other as its anonymous bearers and vessels, bereaved of individual love and hate, thought and feeling reduced to bare sensations and fantasies of pain and pleasure existing only in and for incessant copulations, without apprehension, conflict, or relationship—without human bonds.

By de-individualizing and dehumanizing sexual acts, which thus become impersonal, pornography reduces or removes the empathy and the mutual identification which restrain us from treating each other merely as objects or means. This empathy is an individual barrier to non-consensual acts, such as rape, torture, and assaultive crimes in general.[5] Without such empathy, we are not humane to each other; and finally, as we become wholly solipsistic, our own humanity is impaired. Pornography, thus, is antihuman and antisocial.

If we do not feel empathy, then others are easily relegated beyond the pale, to become merely means. By inviting us to reduce others to sources of sensation, pornography destroys the psychological bonds that bind society. Laws but proclaim and enforce such bonds which must be cultivated before they can be legislated.

By reducing life to varieties of sex, pornography invites us to regress to a pre-moral world, to return to, and to spin out, pre-adolescent fantasies—fantasies which reject reality and the burdens of individuation, of restraint, of tension, of conflict, of regarding others as more than objects of commitment, of thought, of consideration, and of love. These are the burdens which become heavy and hard to avoid in adolescence. By rejecting

[5] Psychologically, things are more complicated. Sadistic acts deny the humanity of the victim, but such acts could not yield pleasure without some initial identification with the victim. The sexual sensation seems to be produced by the process of de-identification which is endlessly repeated. *Total* de-identification (the result, not the process) permits mistreatment of the victim, but that mistreatment does not yield pleasure, and, therefore, does not become an end in itself. Yet from a social viewpoint, these matters can be neglected: any encouragement of de-identification is likely to provoke socially undesirable behavior.

them, at least in fantasy, a return to the pure libidinal pleasure principle is achieved. And once launched by pornography, fantasy may regress to ever more infantile fears and wishes: people, altogether dehumanized, may be tortured, mutilated, and literally devoured.

Such fantasies are acted out whenever authority fails to control or supports the impulses it usually helps to repress or sublimate—when authority permits and encourages the reduction of human beings to mere means: concentration camps become possible when the bond of human solidarity is broken; when inmates are seen merely as obstacles, or as means to accomplishment, or as sources of pleasure and displeasure and not as ends. The failure of authority to punish the public sale or performance of obscene material is, to many minds, a public sanction of dehumanizing fantasies, if not actions.[6]

Pornography de-sublimates: by regressively disowning empathy and identification, by reducing others to objects, it excludes love, affection and any individual relationship, indeed, any human relationship, while it makes sadistic acts possible and even inviting. Once gratification by relations in which others are more than means is precluded, rage against these ungratifying others is generated: they must be made to suffer for having allowed themselves to be made into objects, and yet not becoming

---

[6] The literary *locus classicus* of the sexual fantasy of de-identification is de Sade or, more recently, *l'Histoire de O* by the pseudonymous Pauline Réage. Because they are unfocussed, not institutionalized, and not positively sanctioned, these invitations lead to fewer and less traceable actions than those of the Nazis or the Communists.

objects altogether, claiming somehow to be more, claiming to be human. The sadist's rage at his solitude, at his solipsistic isolation, at his own inability to accept the independent existence of others—to relate to or even love them—is discharged against those who precipitate it by presuming, and thereby demanding what he cannot give. Unprotected by identification they become both the occasion and the target of revenge.

If sadism were directed against a specific human group, such as Jews or Negroes, the libertarian ideologues who now oppose censorship would advocate it. Should we find a little Negro or a Jewish girl tortured to death, her agony carefully taped by her murderers known to be saturated with sadistic, anti-Semitic or anti-Negro literature, most liberals would want the sale of such literature prohibited.[7] (De-identification is often facilitated by actual and putative ethnic differences; but they are not indispensable and are easily replaced, for instance, by a feeling of, or wish for, great superiority over the victims.) Why should humanity as such be less protected than the specific groups which constitute it? That the hate articulated, or the de-identification urged, is directed against humanity in general rather than exclusively against Jews or Negroes makes it as dangerous to more people, and not less dangerous to any.

One need not be a Christian to realize that a society

[7] Ian Brady and Myra Hindley, who murdered 10-year-old Lesley Ann Downey and taped her long agony, professed to be influenced by the sadistic literature found in their home. They were tried in Chester, England (1966).

in which people perceive each other mainly as sources of, or obstacles to, pleasure is not likely to cohere at all. It would lack the identification required for cohesion and, it would exclude love and affection: emotional commitments to persons and not to the impersonal pleasure yielded by them.[8] In their most sublimated form, these commitments are least dependent on impersonal sensations (and on the sources thereof) and most dependent on personal feelings. Feelings cannot be legislated or manufactured; but they can be cultivated. Some cultural climates foster, and others impair them. Laws can protect the cultivation of feelings and penalize what might destroy them. Pornography, in exalting the instrumental use we can make of each other, depreciates and destroys the emotions that go with devotion to or consideration for others, as ends. Yet love and affection are precious—and precarious—heritages of our civilization and their socialized modes, compassion and empathy, are indispensable to it.

To be sure, cultivation of these feelings is not indispensable to all civilizations. In some, a shared concern for something other than one's fellow man, such as survival of the tribe, or fame, or salvation, may altogether take the place of compassion and empathy. This may have been the case in antiquity, and occasionally, in the Middle Ages. But in our culture, such a replacement is unlikely without a return to barbarism, be it sponsored

[8] This is why Freud regarded barriers to the gratification of the sexual impulse as indispensable to the achievement of love. (See his *The Most Prevalent Form of Degradation in Erotic Life.*)

by Communists or Nazis or by more inchoate chiliastic movements.

Shouldn't adults be able to control themselves and be able to read or see what they know to be wrong without enacting it? They should, and some are. But not all. (Incidentally, it is impossible, at least in the American environment, to limit anything to adults; children and adolescents are not supervised enough—and the authority of their supervisors has been too weak for too long.) Too many grownups are far from the self-restrained healthy types envisaged by much libertarian theory. They may easily be given a last, or first, push by obscene literature.

This is no secret. People know that their "spirit is willing but the flesh is weak." They pray they may not be led into temptation. Did they not feel tempted, there would be no problem. Censorship laws are, in the first place, a defense for those who fear temptation: they help restrain impulses of which the actor fears to become a victim before anyone else does. In the second place, censorship laws protect third persons who might be victimized. As are many other laws, censorship laws are enacted because we are enticed—in different degrees—by what they prohibit, and have decided not to yield and, therefore, want to reduce the temptation. Above all, censorship laws proclaim the scope of the social ethos, the social rejection of pornography—however unavoidable the furtive survival of some of it.

In all known societies, people function by controlling their impulses, consciously or semiconsciously, and through unconscious repression. The more unconscious the repression, the more ambivalent they feel about whatever may remobilize what has been repressed. The impulse stirs when stimulated, and so do the defenses. Wherefore, as a matter of psychic economy, people tend to avoid what may upset their equilibrium. And they want the law to help them.

Obscene communications, it is feared, may make it hard, even impossible, to control the cravings they arouse; such cravings are felt by many as threats to the personality integration and Ego dominance they have achieved. It matters not at all whether the loss of control would actually occur. What matters is that *the fear* of losing control does. (It is often projected on others: the fearful person may see them as uncontrolled, himself as victim.) This felt threat arouses enough anxiety in many people to value censorship: censorship functions as the social analogue to individual repression and defense of sublimation. Neither would occur, did it not have necessary functions, which do not become psychologically unnecessary if we demonstrate that they are rationally unneeded. Simply telling a patient what he has repressed and expecting him to deal with it, is, at best, ineffective, at worst, dangerous. The defense—repression—has served a function, and, unless the patient collapses, a defense mechanism will reappear as long as it is needed. So will censorship if we abolish it. But as do defenses, it will reappear in more extreme and sweeping form.

Neither individual repression nor social censorship

are ideal solutions to the problem of anxiety. But we do not live in an ideal world with ideal people. And solutions that ignore the problems people actually have are not helpful. Such solutions may make matters worse: the elimination of legal censorship might well provoke arbitrary and damaging non-legal attempts at repression by private persons and groups—just as stimulations which it cannot handle may bring about sweeping defensive repressions in the individual psyche.

Let me summarize the argument before descending to specifics. Human societies can be analyzed and, up to a point, managed, quite rationally; but they are not held together by reason. Societies are cemented by feelings of human solidarity, compassion, identification and empathy and by shared objects of worship or goals. Some degree of mutual identification is normally acquired or, at least, reinforced in the process of socialization. Mutual identification is further intensified, limited or enlarged by a variety of norms, customs and institutions cultivated in associations which enjoin some version of the golden rule. Part of us always rebels against restraints and sublimations and would use others but as means for our own impulse gratifications. Pornography tends to encourage such regression, and thereby to encourage crime, and above all to weaken human solidarity even among those who stay within the law. Further, pornography tends to erode our cultural heritage by inviting us to desublimate and to sever the link forged in our society between love, or affection (individual feelings for other individuals) and sex (impersonal appeals to the senses).

II

What specific effects can be expected from pornography? Obviously, human action is influenced by communications; else the *Bible, Das Kapital, Mein Kampf,* or *The Sorrows of Young Werther* would have had no impact. Our sexual impulses have not changed; our sexual mores have. They were influenced by ideas and attitudes spread, sometimes even created, by books. So, too, are changes in crime. Books influence what we feel, what we love and hate, indulge or restrain, cultivate or repress, and, finally, what actions we take. They influenced Hitler, Martin Luther King, Jr., and his murderer.

Different personalities are influenced in different ways and degrees by the same books. After all, personalities differ inasmuch as their reaction to the same things differs, owing to different constitution and experience. However, if objects such as books or pictures were not similarly perceived on some level and reacted to in similar ways, they would not be recognized as the same objects. The world would be but projection. Beauty (or obscenity) would, indeed, be in the eye of the beholder. Except for ophthalmic peculiarities, I would not be less beautiful than the current Miss Universe, or my paintings inferior to Leonardo's.[9]

[9] This absurdity is believed because aesthetic qualities are hard to demonstrate; and some people think that whatever is not, or cannot be, demonstrated does not exist or is subjective. But existence, truth, and demonstrability differ as do knowledge and its objects. The subjectivity of knowledge or belief does not infect its object.

Yet, I think there is a relationship, other than identity, between subject and object; the object has some influence on how it is perceived and even reacted to, at least by people in roughly the same culture. Thus, people react similarly: they do not éat books; they read them. And obscene communications tend to be identified, perceived and reacted to in roughly similar ways by most persons—although, of course, there are individual differences, largely of degree. (Very different personalities might read altogether different books though there is usually some overlapping. But even a person who wholly refrains from reading pornographic books is affected by the attitudes and actions of those who do.)

The extent to which reaction to pornography is affected by prior experience (or age, sex and class) is nearly unknown. But it seems as wrong to say "He reads what he reads, *only* because he is what he is," as it is to say "He became what he is, *only* because of what he read." Reading is a variable which influences dispositions and actions, more or less importantly depending on prior and concomitant conditions. Reading may or may not precipitate if not cause (or cause, if not precipitate) action: suicide, homicide, divorce, marriage, wife-swapping, sex murder, bank robbery—or entry into a monastery.

By and large, three reactions to pornography seem likely. Some individuals might be vicariously gratified by pornographic communications, and, perhaps, be stimulated to masturbation. In the absence of pornography,

such persons might find other means of vicarious gratification, or do without. (I do not believe that vicarious
gratification can go far: hunger is intensified, rather than
gratified, by reading about or seeing food.)

A second group of persons might harmlessly emulate
what pornography invites to; or they may harm themselves and their consenting partners; or they may emulate
pornography viciously to the point of criminality.[10] (To
deny this probability is to deny that advertising and books
can influence fashions, purchasing patterns, thoughts and
actions.)[11] My impression is that there are fairly few
habitues in these two groups, although an unknown number of persons may join occasionally.

Most persons do not emulate pornography directly,
or habitually use it to stimulate themselves. Yet pornography has a cumulative influence on the lives of this third
group by affecting public morality and also everybody's
personal attitudes, values and ambitions. Any model of
action attractive to some part of the average person when

[10] It is silly to insist that unless criminal sex acts can be traced directly
to consumption of pornography by the criminal, pornography must be
harmless. Lack of evidence for harmfulness is not evidence for harmless-
ness. Moreover, there is no reason to assume that the de-identification
supported by pornography will directly find sexual outlets. Finally, the
influence of pornography is usually diffuse and often indirect, as is the
case of Marxism or religion.

[11] Of course, advertising does not originate there; nor does pornography. However both can intensify, spread, persuade. Neither would
exist if it did not have some influence which occasionally will go all the
way to imitation, within or outside the law. Cigarette advertising surely
does not cause smoking, but it bestows social sanction on smoking.

presented often enough will influence attitudes and make what is modelled—be it anti-semitic, or sadistic, or Communist—more acceptable. Extolling either martial or pacific virtues will make either of them more acceptable; and so will the inviting presentation of sexual vices. (Obscenely described, sex becomes a vice.)

Those who would not be led into harmful actions by pornography will be deprived of a harmless pasttime if it is outlawed. If others are protected from harm thereby, and if society is, censorship is as justifiable—as a speed limit is, or prohibiting the keeping of lions, however tame, in city apartments.

III

If pornography is undesirable, as I believe to have shown, so are many other things which are not outlawed because, by banning them, we might lose, endanger or impair desirable things. Thus, the problem still to be dealt with becomes: is pornography unavoidable with, or necessary to freedom and art? is it inseparable from either or both, inasmuch as censorship—owing to intrinsic indivisibilities, or to human frailty—could not but be so arbitrary as to do more damage to freedom, or art, than is tolerable, or worth suffering for the sake of outlawing pornography? If not, can censorship reduce the harm that would be done by what it censors enough to offset other costs, and if so, how effective could it be? I think that censorship of pornography need not damage freedom or art or literature; that censorship can be effective and that the advantages would offset the costs.

In hard-core cases it is fairly easy to separate pornography from literature. The material is pornographic if, in the opinion of the deciding body (best, a jury), two of the following three criteria are met: 1) if the pornographic intention is proved by admission, testimony, or circumstances; 2) if the marketing, in the main, is directed at prurient interest; 3) if the prevalent effect is sexual arousal.[12] (Since effects differ, a jury would consult witnesses and its own reactions.)

The difficulties have been greatly exaggerated here. I have yet to meet a person who cannot separate most pornography from most literature.[13]

Consider, then, instances in which one might disagree on intent or effect. Perhaps the effect is prurient, but it cannot be shown that the intent was; or the prurient effect is much less than universal; or it is combined with apparently valuable elements of style or content; or the work is obscene yet not arousing—that is, it is unsuccessful as a stimulant. Here one must keep in mind the aesthetic functions of art and literature which distinguish both from obscene or prurient works. Pornography has one aim only: to arouse the reader's lust. The reader, by sharing the fantasy manufactured for him, is to attain

[12] If the arousal is universal, it is, by definition, impersonal.

[13] It is not surprising that lawyers, for the sake of clients, have invented interpretations which obscure and nullify the statutes; it is surprising, however, that the courts have been so inept in clarifying them and in carrying out the obvious and legitimate intent of the legislators.

a vicarious sexual experience. Literature, however, aims at the contemplation of experience and at the revelation of its significance. Art is not an *Ersatz* experience, nor does it invite direct emulation.[14] If, "high art" does not, as Santayana said, "cancel lust," it also does not aim at arousing[15] it or separating it from content.

Revelation, too, is an experience, but one which helps illuminate and enlarge the possibilities and complexities of the human career, whereas pornography narrows and, simplifies them till they are reduced to a series of more or less sophisticated but anonymous (therefore monotonous) sensations. Artistic and literary experiences are intellectual and emotional in nature: they are perceived through the scenes but experienced as feelings and thoughts,[16] not sensations.

Since it is impossible to serve pornography pure, the vicarious experience it supplies must occur through some medium—words or pictures in a setting that permits the suspension of disbelief. This is as far as the similarity with literature goes. Aesthetic merit would be distracting.

---

[14] Freud, at times, thought of art as a substitute. I have suggested why I think him wrong on this in my "Of Happiness and of Despair We Have No Measure" (Chapt. 19, *Passion and Social Constraint*).

[15] V. Jean Genet (*Playboy,* April, 1954): "I now think that if my books arouse readers sexually, they are badly written because the poetic emotion should be so strong that no reader is moved sexually."

[16] Susan Sontag's fashionably campy attempt to establish pornography as an art form is unconvincing. Note, however, that her instances of pornographic art are all instances of pornographic sadism. When ambitious, pornography usually becomes sadistic without becoming art.

Pornography and literature are mutually exclusive. Pornographers no more produce literature than accountants do, or copywriters. Pornographers avoid distraction by using well-worn and inconspicuous cliches and conventions which do not encumber the libidinous action. Thus, in Joyce or Lawrence the reader's arousal, if it occurs at all, is incidental to the aesthetic experience. And it is in Hubert Selby (*Last Exit to Brooklyn*). To be sure, whatever their intentions these authors may be read by some for the sake of masturbatory fantasy. But the separation from human context and the avoidance of literary experience would not derive from the writers—it would be the reader's doing. Despite his intent to separate them, such a reader might actually benefit by reading what he wants conjoined to what he tries to separate it from.

It is hard to imagine a literary critic actually unable to tell pornography from literature although many pretend to be. What could a critic tell us if he cannot tell pornography from literature? If he is as incompetent as he professes to be, why take him seriously? If he feels that for the sake of freedom he must pretend that he cannot discriminate—just as Communists used to be unable to tell democracy from dictatorship whenever such a distinction would interfere with their ideology—why take the pretention seriously?

Nor is distinguishability impaired by contested or actual borderline cases. Disagreement among experts does not entail an impossibility to judge. There is, indeed, a twilight zone where light and darkness merge; yet they can be distinguished from each other. And the law can draw a fairly clear line, arbitrary only insofar as most things in reality are continuous and must be separated if we wish to distinguish among them. Certainly, the line will be drawn differently at different times and in different places. But if dress changes with fashion, we know at any given time what is or, at least, what is not permissible. So with pornography.

The judgments of the censor, thus, need not be more arbitrary than other judgments. Few cases are likely to be brought to court: most objectionable material is unlikely to be published. Nothing could be lost, for if something has aesthetic value, by definition it cannot be pornography.[17] As for effectiveness, laws, of course, never eliminate what they prohibit; by penalizing, laws, however, reduce the frequency of the prohibited action. Censorship will reduce the accessibility and public nature even of the remaining pornography, and proclaim public disapproval.

IV

Social cohesion rests on shared values, customs and traditions which identify us as members of a society. We are disposed, accordingly, to empathy, cooperation, lawful behavior, and even altruistic acts. We understand each other, for we "speak the same language;" that is, we share the same values, perceptions, identifications,

---

[17] On the loss of diversion, see above (p.157) or apply the *de minimis* rule.

ideals, reactions and rules of action. A social order is both the effect and the cause of shared values and beliefs.

Social cohesion does not extend equally to everybody or require that all hold exactly the same values. There are dissenters and deviants; and they can be useful. But they dissent or deviate from something—the shared values of society. Usually they do so according to shared ideas about dissent and are dealt with according to shared ideas about legitimacy. These shared ideas do change over time and space, but usually in a fairly continuous manner. Social cohesion requires that the central values of a society be held by its leadership and followed by its majority and transmitted and elaborated by its institutions.

Freedom—the range within which the individual can choose values and actions—may be among the shared values of a society. Within any social order, freedom must be balanced against other values when it is in conflict or competition with them (e.g., the freedom and security of others; defense; law enforcement; welfare; efficiency). Unlike welfare, freedom can be used against itself: we can use freedom to abrogate or undermine it. Hence, freedom, unlike most other values, must be limited to continue. Unlimited freedom in communication is as inconsistent with any social order as is unlimited freedom in action. For the former leads to the latter and cannot be as easily separated from it as John Stuart Mill thought. Communication need not be limited to the same degree as action must be. Roughly, the more remote from action it is and the less noxious to central values, the less need to restrict communication.[18]

The mere fact that it erodes social cohesion would be sufficient to prohibit pornography since it is by definition bereft of any aesthetic value which might justify retaining it. Elsewhere, as, perhaps, in India and in Israel, dietary norms are more important than sexual ones. In our society, sexual norms seem important enough to justify prohibition of what is outrageously (and, above all, invitingly) offensive to, and destructive of, this important part of the shared values of our society.

[18] This is a very rough rule. There are cases in which action should be limited less than communication. Thus prostitution and homosexual acts might be as inconsistent with the ethos of a society as is pornography; however, they may be less criminogenic and less infectious. (They tend to appeal to distinctly limited groups.) Further, penalization would inflict considerable suffering on involuntary victims without being very effective. In contrast, the greater and differing damage done by pornography is more easily limited, and censorship inflicts no suffering.

Currently the rabbi of Fairmont Temple in Cleveland, Ohio, and President of the American Jewish Congress, Arthur Lelyveld is also national vice-president of the American Jewish League for Israel.

During the summer of 1964, Rabbi Lelyveld went to Mississippi as a minister-counselor for the Commission on Race and Religion of the National Council of Churches. During that stay he was severely beaten by segregationists.

Rabbi Lelyveld has been deeply concerned with the cause of world peace. He has been outspoken in calling on the Administration to halt the bombing of North Vietnam to take steps at the negotiating table rather than on the battlefield.

A member of Phi Beta Kappa, Rabbi Lelyveld received his A.B. from Columbia University in 1933. He received an M.H.L. from Hebrew Union College in 1939 where he was ordained as Rabbi, and a degree of Doctor of Divinity from the Hebrew Union College.

Arthur Lelyveld

I am against censorship.

This is neither a very brave nor radical statement—especially if one is about to hedge that statement with argument and explanation.

Most Americans are opposed to censorship—especially when they view censorship from a distance. The evil in the limitation of the freedom to speak and to publish, whether the evil lies in the Soviet Union, in Czechoslovakia, or in Greece, is an obvious evil.

Most Americans would also be opposed to any limitation of that freedom in our own country. With one big exception: many are not at all sure how much leeway should be accorded so-called pornography or obscenity.

Doubts are heightened by the fact that a new Restoration Era is in full swing, three centuries after the era when "virgins smiled at what they blushed at before." Today's reaction is against the same excessive Puritanism that prompted the 17th-century rebellion.

Where should the line of prohibition be drawn? Can we, without injuring society, remove all legal restraints and say that anything goes?

This essay will argue that freedom to speak, to publish, or to communicate from stage, screen or any other public media should be subject to only two inhibitions. The first is that which flows naturally from public taste. The people can choose to reject what is offered, to ignore it, or even to condemn it. The second inhibition is that which may result from the provision for after-the-fact, due-process review under carefully drawn laws prohibiting demonstrable injury to human welfare or human rights.

Censorship is something quite different. It is always and everywhere an evil. Censorship means the screening of material by an authority invested with power to ban that which it disapproves. A censor is someone appointed to regulate public morals and judge public taste. And who is that paragon to whom we would be willing to entrust such authority? And who, if he be such a paragon, would be willing to accept the responsibility?

In 1644, John Milton published his *Areopagitica: A Speech for the Liberty of Unlicensed Printing* when printing was the major medium for the dissemination of ideas. Milton's essay should have been the last word on censorship for it limned the dangers with unmatched eloquence:

> . . . *there is not aught more likely to be prohibited than truth itself; whose first appearance to our eyes bleared and dimmed with prejudice and custom, is more unsightly and implausible than many errors. . . .*
>
> *And though all the winds of doctrine were let loose to play upon the earth, so*

> *Truth be in the field, we do injuriously by licensing and prohibiting, to misdoubt her strength. Let her and Falsehood grapple . . .*

What Milton held in defense of the absolute right to publish applies also to judgments about what is obscene and what is not obscene. One man's obscenity is another man's customary mode of expression. In art and in drama, as well as in literature, it is only the arrantly self-certain who would know where to cry halt.

But having enlisted on the side of freedom, we need not slough off the social problems which come in the wake of license. Those who would exploit prurience for profit have been quick to take advantage of the new freedom. American sex movies today are a billion-dollar-a-year business with low costs yielding astronomical profits. The marquees along New York's 42nd Street which advertise "Adult Movies" become more brazen day by day. But compared to the huge nudes on billboards abutting Picadilly Circus which thrust over-sized breasts into the London night, the 42nd Street display looks positively decorous. The four-letter word, long tabooed in polite society, is today a commonplace used even by distinguished professors of theology.

During this last decade, public acceptance of these trends has been deepening with amazing speed. *Portnoy's Complaint* and its genre make *Fanny Hill* and *Lady Chatterley's Lover* look like Sunday School primers.

Only six years ago, poor Nick Jacobellis, manager of a motion picture theatre in Cleveland Heights, Ohio, had to fight all the way up to the Supreme Court for his right to show *The Lovers*, a French film which climaxed in a fleeting but tender scene of sexual intercourse. Jacobellis had been convicted of violating Ohio's obscenity laws. After a long and costly fight, the conviction was reversed. But, today, explicit sex scenes—heterosexual, homosexual and bestial—are a dime a dozen and no one bats an eyelash.

It is all in large part a matter of manners. If in the Restoration Era, Louise de Keroualle titillated her admirers by posing for Lely, the portrait artist, with one breast bared—later, Nell Gwyn "went her one better"—in 1970, the wife of a New England Senator strives for the same effect by appearing at a White House reception in a see-through blouse. We have in all the media—TV, paperback books with "girls on the jackets and no jackets on the girls," magazines, and art books—come a long, long way from Anthony Comstock and *September Morn*.

There is no denying that the new freedom affords a refreshing release from furtiveness and from clandestine "dirtiness." Why, then, are some aspects of this flood of uninhibited expression so offensive? The counter-reaction is being expressed not only by the descendants of *Watch and Ward* but also by impressive public personalities. Recently, a professor of pediatric psychiatry gave voice to his fear that the brutality and the cheapness of current sex displays may diminish the meaning, the loveliness—

and hence the joy—of the future love life of mankind.

D. H. Lawrence, whose *Lady Chatterley's Lover* was a landmark case in the battle against censorship, professed that he himself would censor "real" pornography "rigorously," and for the same reasons as those given by the psychiatrist just referred to. Said Lawrence:

> *Pornography is the attempt to insult sex, to do dirt on it. Take the very lowest instance, the picture postcard sold underhand . . . What I have seen of them have been of an ugliness to make you cry . . . they make the sexual act trivial and cheap and nasty.*

Writing about the era of the Restoration, the Durants said:

> *There was an invigorating frankness, a scorn of hypocrisy, in the literature, the theatre and the court. But the candor released a flood of coarseness . . .*

And many of us, sharing this ambivalence, would concur in the judgment of a *New York Times* editorial writer who characterized pornography as:

> *. . . the literary equivalent of prostitution because it treats human relationship in a*

> *loveless, manipulative and degrading
> fashion.*

But how to deal effectively with such social evils? If absolute freedom to show and tell brings abuses in its train, is censorship a warranted and effective remedy? John Milton said "no" with a trenchant and unforgettable analogy:

> *. . . evil manners are as perfectly learned
> without books a thousand other ways
> which cannot be stopped . . . And he who
> were pleasantly disposed, could not well
> avoid to liken it to the exploit of that gal-
> lant man, who thought to pound up the
> crows by shutting his park gate.*

A helpful distinction is available in the Jewish view of this matter; it is a distinction founded largely on intent. When the ancient rabbis were teaching or expounding the traditional sources, they spoke and wrote with the utmost freedom and frankness, as did the Biblical material on which they based their discussion. But when the intent was to demean, "to do dirt" on sex, to insult sex or deprecate sex, then this was inadmissible coarseness. In Hebrew the phrase used was *nibbul peh:* literally, "disfigurement of the mouth." Says one Talmudic teacher:

> *Everyone knows why the bride is*

> *brought into the bridal-tent, but anyone*
> *who befouls that moment with his mouth,*
> *even if seventy years of good have been*
> *decreed for him, has it changed into*
> *seventy years of evil.*

And this judgment applies with equal force to anyone who *listens* to foul and leering speech and who remains silent.

Note, however, that *the penalty for coarseness is not legal action but moral condemnation.* The text itself speaks with perfect freedom about sexual intercourse. Condemnation falls only on that which is intentionally degrading and lewd.

The Bible contains abundant references to the sex act, homosexual as well heterosexual, to rape, to prostitution, and to fornication. The Bible refers without self-consciousness to natural functions, and the Bible preserves some of the world's most beautiful erotic poetry. It is noteworthy that the same authorities who were banning Rousseau's *Confessions* were putting into the hands of youngsters the story of David and Bathsheba, of Judah and Tamer, and of Lot and the men of Sodom. Had they been consistent they would have banned Chaucer's *Canterbury Tales,* the plays of Ben Jonson, and the works of Shakespeare.

Indeed, as most legal authorities agree, it is impossible to arrive at a reasonable, workable definition of obscenity for purposes of censorship. It is this difficulty that leads many jurists toward an absolutist interpretation of the First Amendment. In the words of Justice Hugo Black:

> *My view is, without deviation, without exception, without any ifs, buts, or whereases, that freedom of speech means that you shall not do something to people either for the views they have, or the views they express, or the words they speak or write.*

In this imperfect world, however, such absolutism exists only as a philosophical ideal. There are penalties for libel, for incitement creating "clear and present danger," and there is protection for military secrets essential to public security. Even Justice Black's absolutism was a new departure for him. In 1942 he sat on a Supreme Court case and concurred in a unanimous decision written by Justice Frank Murphy and containing this expression of limitation:

> *There are certain well-defined and narrowly limited classes of speech, the prevention and punishment of which have never been thought to raise any constitutional problem. These include the lewd and obscene, the profane, the libelous, and the insulting or 'fighting' words.*

But Justice Black may have come to see the difficulty of making the necessary legal distinctions that would make possible a defensible definition of what is obscene and what is not obscene. Thus, in a 1970 challenge to the constitutionality of Michigan's obscenity law, the plaintiff's brief contended that the definition of obscenity is "so vague, fluid and indefinite that men of common intelligence must necessarily guess at the meaning and differ as to the application."

Freedom of expression, if it is to be meaningful at all, must include freedom for "that which we loathe," for it is obvious that it is no great virtue and presents no great difficulty for one to accord freedom to what we approve or to that to which we are indifferent.

This is the heart of the dilemma. That which I hold to be true has no protection if I permit that which I hold to be false to be suppressed—for you may with equal logic turn about tomorrow and label my truth as falsehood.

The same test applies to what I consider lovely or unlovely, moral or immoral, edifying or unedifying. This is why, Milton Konvitz tells us:

> *The invaluable and the valueless, the noble and the tawdry, the beautiful and the ugly, the true and the false, the good and the evil, are equally protected by the First and the Fourteenth Amendments' guarantees of a free press and religious*

liberty.

But, praised be the law, this same freedom makes possible our right to condemn, to decry and to attack, as effectively as we can, that which is in our view tawdry or salacious or nauseating. To affirm freedom is not to applaud that which is done under its sign. Thomas Jefferson showed vigor and indignation as he made this point:

> *I deplore . . . the putrid state into which our newspapers have passed, and the malignity, the vulgarity, and the mendacious spirit of those who write them . . . These ordures are rapidly depraving the public taste.*
>
> *It is, however, an evil for which there is no remedy: Our liberty depends on the freedom of the press and that cannot be limited without being lost.*

Jefferson, a master stylist, uses the word *ordures,* and any person of taste—my taste, of course—will approve the elegance of that choice as against the Anglo-Saxon synonym which he eschewed. The meaning and the reference, however, are the same.

But I have a right to want the law to prevent you from *imposing* your "ordures" on me. The law cannot create morality and taste, but it can prevent you from rubbing my nose in what I consider to be execrable. This is what Oliver Wendell Holmes, Jr., meant when he said "my right to swing my arm ends at the point at which your nose begins." It should be added that our new devices for instantaneous and universal communication make "your arm" far longer than it used to be, and it may well be necessary for legal authorities to give careful consideration to whether or not an extension of the doctrine of "clear and present danger" is required. The dissemination of a slogan like "Off the pigs!" in Portland, Oregon, may not be totally unrelated to the killing of a policeman in Cleveland, Ohio. This is the obverse of a statement made by Judge Curtis Bok in an opinion rendered in a 1949 case:

> *If speech is to be free anywhere it must be free everywhere . . . What is said in Pennsylvania may clarify an issue in California.*

This is a valid reflection which works both ways. What is said in Pennsylvania may produce a clear and present malign result in California. But this is a complex question filled with unsuspected dangers, and it had best be studied by the most competent constitutional authorities.

Ignored in the hullaballoo about the report of the Commission on Obscenity and Pornography is the fact that the Commission has recognized this dilemma, and has affirmed the propriety of legislative action to protect the individual's right to make his own choices as to what he wishes to see and to hear. Its majority report includes this declaration:

> *Certain explicit sexual materials are capable of causing considerable offense to numerous Americans when thrust upon them without their consent. The commission believes that these unwanted intrusions upon individual sensibilities warrant legislative regulation and it further believes that such intrusions can be regulated effectively without any significant interference with consensual communication of sexual material among adults.*

If this is an acceptable limitation, then it is certainly *a fortiori* true, as the Commission recognizes, that "explicit sexual materials," particularly those that brutalize and insult sex, should not be thrust upon children. But here we are desperately confused. It is possible to be degradingly lewd while fully clothed. I would rather my own children saw *The Lovers* than have had them see the late Marilyn Monroe in *Some Like It Hot,* a movie in which adultery and transvestitism were leering jokes. Many motion pictures rated for general audiences seem to me far more harmful than many that are rated "Restricted."

And this is where we came in. Legislation will not

lighten the complexity of these problems, and censorship will not solve them. We can but hope that more and more men will come to have respect for human life and for the potentialities of human relationship. And as for that which is depraved and disgusting in our own time, we can only wait for taste and good judgement to reassert themselves after the first wild release.

Fortunately, there is some evidence that pornography has its own cure built into it—after a relatively short time pornography produces ennui. Those exposed to it, according to Dr. James Howard who carried out some of the experimental work of the Commission on Obscenity, "quickly became satiated and bored." As boredom sets in, nudity and pornography will become less profitable for its panderers.

Repression, on the other hand, as the Prohibition experiment showed us, creates an unwholesome, heightened desire for that which is forbidden. No one bothers to write a crudity on a wall or on a placard exposed to public view unless such a writing is considered banned and appropriate only to secret places, such as the cubicle of a men's room.

It isn't easy. But I have seen freedom and I have seen repression. Freedom is better.

Max Lerner, author, teacher and journalist, is currently pro-fessor of American Civilization and World Politics at Bran-deis University. As a journalist and scholar, he has traveled to almost every part of the world, and has lectured before uni-versity groups on six continents.

His newspaper column, which he writes three times a week, appears in the NEW YORK POST, *and is widely syndicated both in the United States and internationally.*

Mr. Lerner has written a dozen books, of which the best known is AMERICA AS A CIVILIZATION. *His most recently pub-lished book is* TOCQUEVILLE AND AMERICAN CIVILIZATION.

Max Lerner

FOR ME THE PRIMARY QUESTION revolves around neither pornography nor censorship—both of which have a history, a beginning, and probably an ending—but around the more permanent themes of the erotic and the creative. I put a double question as a frame for this essay: How do you get the freedoms—and, perhaps, also the restraints—necessary for erotic fulfillment? And how do you get the kind of literary and artistic creativeness which feeds on the erotic imagination? Whatever importance either pornography or censorship may have derives from this context.

To start with the erotic: America is moving toward an expanding sexual freedom, as no great society in history (not even the Roman Empire nor Louis XIV's) has done in so brief a period, on so vast a scale. The admission price that any social critic must pay for the right to make sense of the pornography question is the effort to grasp the full dimension of the current sexual revolution in America. The breakthrough of the erotic word and image is an aspect not of the political but of the sexual revolution.

There are things about the revolution we may dislike, but we ignore it as a whole only at our peril. The history of mankind offers us only a handful of such eras of revolutionary sexual liberation: the Alexandrian age,

Rome under the early emperors, the civilization of India at the time of the Konarak sculptures, the Renaissance in Italy, England under the Restoration, Islam under the Ottoman emperors, France in the Revolutionary era, and America and Western Europe in the post-Freud and post-Kinsey climate. I venture to say that in none of the earlier cases has a civilization been shaken up *to its very foundations* as ours has been in the past quarter century in its revolt against long-standing sexual taboos.

This sexual revolution is, in turn, part of a larger cultural revolution, shaking up not only moral, legal, and religious codes, but whole value systems—in fact, the life-style of the cultures affected. We have given it a name—the "counter-culture" or "adversary culture"—to signify how far and how deep it reaches: into new uses of old drugs; a new profile of clothes, hair, and body style for women and men alike; new freedoms in spoken and written language; a new openness in plays and movies and in the pictorial and plastic arts; new casualness about sexual behavior; new forms of "sensitivity training" and "total encounter" therapy, and thus new psychologies; a return to earlier mysticisms; new experiments with communitarian colonies; new attitudes toward the family and marriage; new attitudes toward all forms of authority, including that of war and its establishments; a new behavior in the classrooms and on the campuses; and a new assertion of women's ancient grievances, with a more thoroughgoing drive to achieve women's equality—de jure and de facto—than, perhaps, ever in any historical society.

Given this larger revolutionary frame bearing on the erotic and creative life, it should be clear how limited censorship is as a concept, and how frail it must prove as a functioning check. It is an instrument conceived by moralists, given precision by lawyers, carried out by bureaucrats. It once had a chance of working in the tight community of a church-controlled society, and it may still work tolerably in a soldier-controlled garrison state or in a bureaucrat-controlled Communist state knit together by a dogmatic political religion. In such societies the aim of censorship is politico-military-religious: it is to protect the gods of the temple, the family and the tribe, and thus protect the foundations of the state from enemies without and within.

But in societies like the American and West European where the dynamics of energy come from freedom and where the climate and the whole ethos are those of freedom, censorship is bound to be at worst, stupid; at best, futile; and always, to some degree, unconsonant with the character of the society as a whole. The effort to legislate and censor pornography out of existence has curiously been sustained longest in England and America, aside from the Catholic Church's *Index* and its efforts to control lewdness and blasphemy in print. Many commentators have tended to ascribe this to the Puritan background in the Anglo-Saxon countries; and there is little question that—notably in the case of D. H. Lawrence—the rhetoric of the crusading writers has been anti-Puritan. But this explanation strikes me as pretty rickety since it doesn't explain why the French and the Swiss and the Germans with their Calvinist and Lutheran heritages have not been as pre-occupied with the struggle against pornography.

A more promising approach is through the norm-setting classes. As long as the aristocracies managed to set the norms of dress, gentility, literature, the arts, education, and moral codes, the force of their example was strong enough to awe the underlying population, and teach them either to keep their distance or to seek to imitate. But when the middle classes came into power— as they did, first and most strongly, in England and America, partly in linkage with the Puritan economic virtues—the middle classes became norm-setting as well. This was particularly true in America which never had a feudal aristrocracy of any importance to overthrow. America moved rapidly into the era of rootless and norm-less Megalopolis, with religious ties broken, and with equality as the sail, and with only freedom as the rudder.

My own commitment to freedom doesn't make censorship an absolute for me. I recognize the pragmatic possibility that censorship will be needed in a war. During such a time, every nation, without exception, has used censorship. Anyone sending a dispatch from Israel or from an Arab country finds the censor a reality. There is no formal censorship for American reporters in Vietnam, but there is an informal and self-imposed code of restraints observed by most of them, which is probably as it should be.

Far more serious is the report—doubtless authentic —that the Nixon Administration has in readiness a censorship setup in the event of nuclear attack. The nation will be divided into censorship areas, and a group of central censors (already named secretly) will operate out of a deep underground shelter in the Maryland area. One of their functions may be to prevent panic on the nation's roads and in the big cities by "managing" the news of the attack. This raises extraordinary questions about news management, always a subtle form of thought manipulation and therefore of censorship; but an era with nuclear weapons is bound to be an extraordinary era. What troubles me is not the coming secret authority of the censors, but the current secrecy about that secrecy.

One trouble with censorship as a concept is its portmanteau character, covering all forms of writing, speaking, and reading, all art forms, and various aspects of sexual behavior and display. The crucial divide, for me, is between political and moral censorship, between the effort to control dangerous opinions and thoughts, and the effort to control the erotic and pornographic in expression. The first is the area of power, and—except for wartime and the marginal "clear and present danger" that Holmes spoke of—the confrontation between power and freedom. A society that values freedom can make no other choice here than that of freedom.

What censorship seeks to protect in this primarily political area may be, in wartime, the very existence of the nation; in peacetime, it is more likely to be a particular vested interest, or the power of a particular power structure. Hence, the strong burden is always on the authorities to prove that some utterance of speech or press or other publication must have limits placed around it: to keep the histrionics of press and media from encroaching on a fair trial; to protect the individual against libel or slander, and (in an era of potential demagogy of the big media) against group defamation; and generally, to protect the individual from invasions of his privacy. In all these cases, the need for some exercise of censorship limits the area of freedom. Yet all the cases are marginal, and the freedom principle must be the dominant principle.

It is the second area, not of power but of Eros, that is far harder to wrestle with. First, because the need for freedom doesn't seem as urgent here as in the political area where a democracy cannot operate unless it can count on a competition of ideas, programs, and potential leaders. Secondly, because the nerve touched by the blatantly erotic and pornographic—the nerve of protecting one's home and children, and insulating them against the dangers of moral contamination and corruption—is a more sensitive nerve than that of political power. Let it be noted that the intellectual elites are most strongly against censorship in both areas: the people—both middle-class and working class—are not. Most of them believe that "license" in speech and press is dangerous, and they link it with the threat of revolution. Even more

of them believe that society must fight against the pollution of the newsstand and the bookstore as much as one
fights against the pollution of air and water. Thus on a
question of denying a license to a burlesque house, a
New York judge spoke of society's "constant vigil to keep
the reservoir clean."

It is easy to mock the people who feel thus. But to
mock them is to forget the religious, the peasant, and the
working class roots of most of the people who today make
up Heartland America, many of them descended at only
one or two removes from the varied ethnic stocks who
came from central and southern Europe. They have
"made it" in America by hard work and by saving and
by sacrifice, and they don't want to see the structure they
helped build torn down by political extremisms or undermined by moral looseness. This is obvious; but the neglect
of the obvious by the intellectual elites makes the struggle
for freedom in the political area more difficult as well.
Unless we understand this aspect of Heartland America,
we shall have only a glimmer of the abiding strength of
various private, but strongly-knit, agencies operating as
pressure groups on both booksellers and public officials,
sometimes with an ill-concealed suggestion of vigilantist
crackdown.

This makes another difference between political and
erotic censorship: the first is usually the work of officials
wishing to protect their ruling elite and keep their power
from being challenged; the second (except in the case of
the powerful churches) is the work of the people them-

selves. When Lyndon Johnson appointed a Commission on Obscenity and Pornography it was because of pressures on and from Congress. Like other harassed Presidents, Johnson didn't know what to do with such pressures, and so he passed the buck back to Congress and the Presidential Commission which was authorized in 1967 and which completed its Report in 1970.

Alan Robbe-Grillet guesses that the people clamor for erotic censorship because they don't want the act of sex to lose its penumbra of mystery and sin, if not of sanctity. It is an ingenious guess, but my own guess would be that the people clamor for censorship because they sense the threat of unbridled sexuality to their whole ethos, and therefore to their whole universe. The liberals, who have made a mystique of "the people" and the will of the comman man on political matters, show a deep contempt for "the people" in the role of conserver of mores.

I don't. I respect whatever it is that makes the middle classes want to hold on to their universe. This doesn't mean that I won't oppose them. For their universe may not be mine, nor their hierarchy of values mine. But I refuse to sneer at them as does Mrs. Grundy or treat them as troglodytes. In the end, their "tread lightly" caveats may be healthier for American survival than the "sweep-everything-away-and-uproot-everything" urgencies of my intellectual, liberal colleagues.

When the U.S. Senate in October, 1970, voted overwhelmingly to reject the findings of the Commission on

Obscenity and Pornography, its Chairman, Dean William B. Lockhart, told the press that "the Senators should have read the Report more carefully." Some of them did—but this misses the point. The Senate vote was not an intellectual appraisal of the Commission's Majority Report: that had been made by the dissenting members, and in the case of several of them—notably that of Morton Hill and Winfrey Link—the counter-report has more intellectual force than some of the Commission's staff work which it takes to pieces. The Senate did not render a book review but a world view, utterly different from the world view of the Commission.

Caught between the two world views, I refuse to swallow either of them. I take what I regard as the only sensible view for an individual: that other persons, like myself, should have open to them the moral choice about the kind of erotic lives they will live, the kind of print they will read, the kind of enactments on stage and screen and elsewhere they will take the trouble to see; but also—since perforce we find ourselves living together in the same society—that I am willing to accept not intolerable limits to this free choice of mine, so that others, with their own kind of ethos, will not be compelled to live in what for them might be an intolerable milieu.

Finally, together we should keep from atomizing the social bonds that connect people with each other, and make society the going organism it is.

If, indeed, Eros is not only sexuality but the whole life-giving and life-expressing principle, then it cannot function when every person, solipsistically, makes an imperative out of his particular hedonist and moral universe. Eros must have a going, thriving society to function in.

I have said that I am willing to accept not intolerable social limits to my own free choice. This is the nub, of course, from a legal standpoint. I have written my share of commentaries on American constitutional decision-making, and am not innocent of what the judicial process is like when nine judges at the apex of the judicial pyramid get together to decide whether a book or a movie is too pornographic to get by the canon. Justice Hugo Black, serene in his conviction that erotic freedom—like political—is part of freedom of press and utterance, will have nothing to do with the headaches that go with the process of drawing a line. But the other judges, in varying degrees, go along with Justice Holmes' general proposition about any body of law without absolutes—that while it is hard to draw a line, "a line there must be."

So they slog along, grimly reading the books in question, wading through the trial records of the courts below, trying to decide what goes and what doesn't. The lines they draw and the tests they use keep shifting, as indeed they must: What is "prurient" or "patently offensive" enough to offend the "ordinary reader" and the going moral code? What will hurt or not hurt children and innocents? What is the offending passage like in its context and in the context of the book as a whole? Does the book or play or picture have some serious artistic merit, or "some redeeming social value," or is it "hard-core pornography"? And even if it has some merit or value—I cite the shaky opinion of Justice Brennan in the Ginzburg case—has its distribution been so commercialized as to infect the source?

There is a hypnotic appeal in this, as there is in all legal and codal casuistry, whether of the medieval Canon Law or in that of the Jewish Talmudic scholars. If a man once gave himself to it, he could sink in the morass. The Court must, I suppose, see it through; although the more sophisticated judges probably see through it even while they take part in the whole mummery. When you read the abler books in this legal area, whether Charles Rembar's on the side of greater freedom or Richard Kuh's on the side of greater restraint, you get the feeling that the Supreme Court judges are caught in an inescapable bind. What they do represents an effort at the top to keep the men at the base of the judicial and administrative pyramid—the state Attorney-Generals, the District Attorneys, the lower courts, the local magistrates, the prosecutors, the police chiefs—from becoming petty and cruel tyrants, and lording it over chaos. The important thing for the Supreme Court is not what rule it adopts but that it should adopt some sort of rule—provided it is a workable one. I suppose it is unlikely to get a much better one than the test of whether the work in question has some literary merit or social value. The added (Ginzburg case) nuance about commercial intent strikes me as both superfluous and unworkable.

I view the Court's efforts not so much with approval or disapproval as with compassion. Its effort is herculean and almost hopeless, for given the revolution of erotic freedom, it is like trying to push back the onrushing flood. I can only wish the Court good luck and a good climate for drawing lines and getting them reasonably enforced.

I don't like censors, and I regard all censorship from without as banal and vulgar, even if some of the effects may be titillating to the imagination. The world of the judges cannot usually be a highly diverting one, although sometimes (as Charles Rembar points out in his account of the British trial of *Lady Chatterley's Lover*) it can be knowingly ludicrous. In such a trial where the writers appear not as writers but as appendages of expertise, their largely intuitive appraisals of a book as literature or nonliterature can sometimes emerge as a non-event.

The only time I ever appeared as expert witness for a book on trial was not before a judge but before the Brooklyn Grand Jury in the case of *Tropic of Cancer,* its author Henry Miller, and its publisher Barney Rossett. It was a good experience for me since it brought me face to face with the people whose psychic energy furnishes the motive force for censorship. The foreman made me feel at home by telling me he was a reader of my column in the New York *Post* and a number of other jurors joined him in his confession. Thus, from the start, I learned something that most critics miss: these were not yokels or illiterate boobs or any other abstraction you can dismiss. They were my neighbors; in fact, my readers. My problem was to persuade them that I was, in turn, an admiring reader of Miller's books, not because he wrote filth but because his books contained a vision of life; that Miller wrote *Cancer* as he did because he was rebelling against the conventional novel and its conventional story-line and its neat, tidy language, and the ways of living that the sweating mass of humanity had always been part of.

I am not sure how well I succeeded. It couldn't have been an utter failure, because the indictment wasn't pushed, and Miller stayed out of jail. I was not, I fear, functioning that morning as a wholly detached literary or social critic. In the language fashionable these days in radical academia, where (as Stanley Diamond insists about anthropologists) "there can only be partisans," I was a partisan. I was not just evaluating a book and its impact on me: I was trying to sell it to the jurymen as being within the canon law. Erotic? Yes! Pornographic? No! (With D. H. Lawrence it was obscenity, yes; pornography, no.)

I deplore the role because I happen to think that a writer betrays himself either as salesman or revolutionary guerilla. Yet the federal judges have also been cast in false roles. Reading the efforts of judges trying to be literary critics—even the best of them, like Woolsey or Frankfurter or Charles E. Clark—one is left with the impression that they are pretty much at sea in stormy weather, striving desperately to keep afloat by hanging onto a life raft thrown to them by those whom they regard as enlightened critics. This is probably where we writers come into the censorship picture: when we testify, it is not really the jurymen and jurywomen we are addressing, but the judges. And it is the judges who are listening, and not the juries. The judges look to the critics for their literary guidelines; but if the critics are wise, they will burn away the indifference they have usually had toward the erotic life-experience of the people themselves, whether liberating or repressive.

The most diverting and perhaps valid defense of erotic censorship I have come upon is one by Robbe-Grillet: that it sharpens the resourcefulness of writers (one might say this as well about political censorship), and that it invests the sexual act with mystery, difficulty, distance. But it is not the censor who thus invests the sexual act: it is the human psyche itself. Apart from some animals, says Robert Graves, "the sexual act is always performed in utter secrecy simply because when one is engaged in it, one becomes very vulnerable." He concludes that because of this inherent secrecy, talk about sex—with anyone except the one you love—is anti-human.

One gets very little sense of such insights in the already hackneyed approach of uncritical sexual liberals who are determined to find that there is no relation between immersion in explicit public sexual material and the posture of the mind that is thus immersed. The staff and majority of the Commission on Obscenity and Pornography may be wrong or right in their conclusions that there is "no evidence to date" of a "significant role" played by explicit sexual material in criminal behavior or in any other social ills; but the Hill-Link dissent which retraverses the same data gives (I quote from a perceptive piece by Murray Kempton) "a most convincing portrait of a commission majority which winnowed the chaff that gave scientific color to its thesis from the chaff that might bring it into dispute."

The Commission's work seems to have been too hastily farmed out, assembled, and organized to give us much notion of what a sustained, in-depth study might come up with.

I don't exclude the physiology of the sexual act from the realm of objective study: the Masters-Johnson first volume must command respect, if not empathy, while their volume on therapy for sexual inadequacies may well have opened new possibilities for helping people with knowledge and advice. I am only sceptical about what social science research, with all its new precision and computer techniques, can do in lighting up the dark places in human erotic feeling, and in measuring the consequences of setting censorship limits around total exposure in literature and the arts—especially the performing arts. Here Montaigne's scepticism—*Que sais-je?*—might prove appropriate.

What indeed do we or can we know, other than conjecture, intuition, and (let us hope) informed insight? Replying to George Steiner's brilliant essay arguing that pornography hurts literature and dehumanizes life by stripping the human being naked of the protective sheath he has placed around sexual privacy and mystery, Maurice Gerodias argues in turn that it is only erotic man who is truly human—that man emerges over the centuries from the animal only when he breaks away from sex *as reproduction* to sex *as pleasure*. The aim of the current sexual revolution is, indeed, as I have especially watched it during the past decade, to reach the hedonic by stripping away all taboos. But while this leads doubtless to social liberation in the sense of greater individual freedom of choice in sexual exposure and action, I wonder whether this also leads to greater humanity, or even to collective security and to the health of society.

We come back here to the great theme that Freud wrestled with—the theme of whether repression (of overt sexuality, of violent urges) is built into civilization, causing its "discontents," yet is necessary to civilization. Freud thought it was, and cited the incest ban as the prime example. The Freudian Left has disagreed, and tends to equate sexual repression with capitalism, ignoring conveniently the sexual Puritanism of the Soviet and the Chinese regimes. In America the movements for political and cultural revolutions have held each other at arm's length; yet there can be little doubt that each has also fed the pace and intensity of the other. Both are in turn part of a much larger movement—world-wide—the undercutting of all symbols of authority, the crumbling of the cement that holds society together. The removal of taboo after taboo has meant a pervasive release of the unconscious, with results for the fragile organism we call "society" that are still incalculable.

Within this far-reaching frame, much of the usual discussion of concrete issues of censorship seems almost trivial, yet such discussion may turn out to be more important than it seems. We seem to be moving inevitably toward the removal of all bans on the written word, although I should myself argue that this should be a gradual, not a sudden, enactment. In the performing arts, which are basically public—movies, theater, TV, public displays—some line should be drawn between what may be done in private and what may be shown in public.

The Commission on Pornography, for example, stayed clear of studying performances of public copulation, yet that, too, must be grappled with. If the basic theory about removing all taboos is valid, can we stop short of any portrayal, including pederasty, incest, group sexual relations, and indeed sexual sadism?

By this logic we cannot stop short of where De Sade stopped, which was nowhere—and which suggests only that this logic is the wrong one for a society as fragile, as vulnerable to violence and disintegration as ours is today.

Blue movies may well have some role in the privacy of one's home, one's own room. But the same portrayals on a screen or a stage, simulated or "real," watched by an audience of strangers in public, raise questions that cannot be dismissed simply by calling for the destruction of taboos.

In the end, of course, social restraints are less important than self-restraint, and public censorship less effective than that of the inner censor. But if all social restraints go, how can we expect self-restraint to be achieved, since self-restraint is only the internalizing of what we find around us in our growing-up years? How develop the inner censor, without which there can be no social contract, if "anything goes" in the public display of the deepest and most primal relations between human beings?

No, Eros in its creative inner core cannot thrive if the outer censor is obtrusive and repressive, for Eros depends on freedom. But it is also true that Eros cannot thrive unless somehow enough of the inner censor remains to give the individual a frame of some sort, and to give society an ethos.

Charles Rember is internationally known as the lawyer principally responsible for the turnabout in the laws regarding obscenity in literature in the United States. Beginning with the LADY CHATTERLEY *case in 1959, continuing with* TROPIC OF CANCER *in 1964 and with* FANNY HILL *in 1966, he induced the Supreme Court to practically nullify its former position concerning the banning of books. The results of his labors were set forth in* THE END OF OBSCENITY *work which was widely reviewed and acclaimed.*

Mr. Rembar has been practicing law in New York City since 1947. He was graduated from Harvard College, and received his LLB from Columbia University Law School.

His articles have appeared in THE ANTIOCH REVIEW, CO-LUMBIA LAW REVIEW, *and* EVERGREEN REVIEW; *his book reviews have been published in* THE NEW YORK SUNDAY TIMES *and* LIFE *magazine.*

Charles Rembar

IN SEVEN YEARS between 1959 and 1966, the language up to then unfit to print became entirely fit. This language was recognized as words, nothing more, not amulets; courts reamed the magic out of them. The power of decision moved from judge and jury to the writer.

More: the revolution went to substance. Thoughts, feelings, scenes, events, whose portrayal and communication the law had theretofore proscribed, could now be set forth plainly. Even this: the reader could be roused. It would not matter, legally, that in reading he, or even she, might suffer—or enjoy—"a genital commotion."[1]

There was a qualification: the book must have some value. But the value need not be large; it could be a modicum. Only writing "utterly without" value might be suppressed. In the climactic case of *Memoirs* v. *Massachusetts,* the case on *Fanny Hill,* the highest court of Massachusetts insisted a book need not "be unqualifiedly worthless before it can be deemed obscene." The

The content of this article appears, in somewhat different form, in the author's book *The End of Obscenity* (Random House, 1968) and in *Censorship and Freedom of Expression: Essays on Obscenity and the Law* (Edited by Harry Clor; Rand McNally, 1971).

[1] This perfect phrase—sonorous Latin precision invoking imagery more commonly expressed in words of Anglo-Saxon origin—is from the pen of Father Harold Gardiner, S. J., author of what to my mind was the best pro-censorship book, *Catholic Viewpoint on Censorship* (Doubleday, 1958), until the appearance of Harry Clor's *Obscenity and Public Morality* (University of Chicago Press, 1969).

Supreme Court declared that this was in error. Pornography, so far as the law was concerned, was no longer a condemnatory word. Indeed, one of the witnesses for its publisher had called *Fanny Hill* "a classic of pornography." The First Amendment stood in the way of anti-obscenity legislation; the statutes could not reach a book unless it was utterly lacking in value.

And value, for the purpose of this rule, included literary merit. Hence a book that had some literary merit could not now be suppressed, no matter how sexually exciting it might be, or how offensive, no matter how lewd, lecherous, libidinous, lascivious, lubricitous, salacious or indecent—or in the most important of the familiar legal synonyms, no matter how lustful. Or in their more recent, somewhat narrower counterpart, no matter how prurient.

So in its traditional, its time-dishonored sense—the impermissible description of sex in literature—the legal concept of obscenity was at an end. Assuming the writer could produce something not "utterly without" merit, which is the same as assuming he was a writer at all, he and his book would be safe. If he had any talent, and if he was making any effort to employ that talent—whatever springs and urges might have put him to work—the law would never bother him. That was the meaning of the *Fanny Hill* case. Literary censorship was gone.

Publishers and booksellers might still be made to observe certain restraints. Where the issue was a close one, smirking wise-guy advertising might get them in trouble; this is the "pandering" doctrine of the much over-publicized *Ginzburg* case, a case that produced a chorus of anguish from libertarian commentators, but provided only negligible comfort to frustrated prosecutors. And sales to minors might be prohibited; this being established, by one of history's charming coincidences, in the *Ginsberg* case. But neither of these peripheral decisions would permit the suppression of a book. And neither would have any significant effect upon the writing of books.

Literary censorship has its most important impact not on the publisher or the bookseller, but on the author. If he must keep an eye to the law, we are deprived of his best efforts. That perversion of the creative process had been stopped. From the time of the Supreme Court's *Fanny Hill* decision in the spring of 1966, no book has been suppressed. Courts would turn attention now to other forms of expression, to media other than the printed word on pages bound together.

*   *   *

This essay, designed as one in a collection, will confine itself to books. It offers no prescriptions or predictions with respect to other kinds of art. But let me suggest two considerations that may be pertinent.

The first resides in opportunity for choice—the voluntary spectator versus one who has the spectacle thrust upon him. *Tropic of Cancer* published as a book is not the same as *Tropic of Cancer* spelled out on billboards. The right to express oneself freely, explicit in the Constitution, may collide with other rights, among them, probably implicit in the Constitution, a general right to be let alone. Privacy in law means various things; and one of the things it means is protection from intrusion. The person who chooses not to read, or not to listen, or not to see, should be allowed to exercise that choice. Anti-obscenity legislation has constitutional room to operate where the audience is captive. The public-address system, the poster, the advertising display, performance in a public park or on the streets—these may validly be regulated.

The second has to do with action and expression. The Amendment protects the latter, not the former; the most liberal of our Justices have insisted on the difference. Not all communication is expression, pure and only. There are activities, including certain art forms, that combine elements of expression and of action.

It is not enough to say the effort is to communicate. The poor soul in the classic arrest for indecent exposure could also say—if it occurred to him—that his effort was to communicate. And no doubt it was. But his "communication" involves conduct that allows the law to intervene without hindrance from the Constitution. Expression as such must be altogether free of governmental intervention, but control of conduct is the proper business of government. It is, indeed, what government is all about. Where action and expression join, the courts must first decide which element, for the purpose at hand, predominates.

These distinctions are likely, I believe, to affect the courts' decisions on other forms of art, but they have no direct bearing on literary censorship. Books are pure expression. Reading a book is a private affair. We are not talking about billboards, or skywriting, or that ubiquitous, intrusive medium, television.[2]

How did our literary censorship get started? How did we get rid of it? Will we stay rid of it? Is it good or bad that we are rid of it?

Censorship is ancient, but censorship for obscenity is not. Indeed, the law of obscenity is hardly three centuries old, a life span brief indeed in Anglo-American law. It began so late in history because there were not many books until late in history. Literary censorship is an elitist notion: obscenity is something from which the masses should be shielded. We never hear a prosecutor, or a condemning judge (and rarely a commentator) declare his moral fiber has been injured by the book in question. It is always someone else's moral fiber for which anxiety is felt. It is "they" who will be damaged. In the seventeenth century, "they" began to read; literacy was no longer confined to the clergy and the upper classes. And it is in the seventeenth century when we first

[2]At the date of writing (July, 1970) it appears that the Supreme Court next fall will deal with the encounter between motion pictures and anti-obscenity legislation in cases arising from the motion picture *I Am Curious (Yellow)*. The distinctions mentioned may play a part in argument and decision. The Court ought to consider that a theatre is not an open place, that the audience is voluntary, not captive. It ought also to observe that the most reasonable and sympathetic object of anti-obscenity legislation—the protection of children—is more practicable with films than with books: the exclusion of children from theatres is readily accomplished, while the imprisonment of easily-transferred books is not.

begin to hear about censorship for obscenity.[3]

There was obscenity censorship in seventeenth-century England, but there was no law of obscenity. Printing was a licensed privilege; it was a simple matter for the government to prevent the publication of any book deemed, by those who happened at the time to constitute the government, objectionable. This is censorship in the narrowest sense: suppression in advance. Since censors, unlike judges, feel no need to explain their actions, or to develop principles that will govern their use of power, no rules of law were stated.

Licensing of printing disappeared from England at the end of the seventeenth century, and has never existed in the United States. But shortly after licensing ended, the English courts decided that publishing an obscene book was a common law crime, that is, an act pronounced criminal by the courts though not prohibited by any statute.[4]

---

[3]The preoccupation of enforcement officials, in the 1950's, with paperbacks as distinguished from hardcover books is a manifestation of the same attitude. Norman Mailer's *The Naked and the Dead,* for example, had few problems with anti-obscenity laws until it came out in paperback. If the prosecutors had succeeded in their selective enforcement of the law, and if we should descend into another economic depression, we might find one-third of a nation ill-fed, ill-housed and with its prurient interest insufficiently appealed to.

[4]The theory of the common law is that it incorporates usage, practice and tradition—customary rules that have always existed, or in any event have existed so long that "man's memory runneth not to the contrary." It probably would have startled Alfred, Edward the Confessor and even Henry II to learn that the use of Anglo-Saxon words for sex was a breach of the King's Peace. Some traditions seem to lie around unnoticed for a long while.

The threat of prosecution was enough to drive a book underground. Neither the author nor the original publisher of *Fanny Hill* was brought to court, but the book disappeared from public view.[5]

The cases that did go to court contributed little to doctrine. A criminal case does not ordinarily carry a judicial opinion unless there is an appeal; and in obscenity prosecutions, there were very few appeals until well into the nineteenth century.

The English common law was adopted by the courts of the United States, and with it the rule that obscenity was criminal. In 1815, in Philadelphia, there was a conviction of certain entrepreneurs who exhibited a painting "representing a man in an obscene, impudent and indecent posture with a woman." The first reported decision on literary censorship came six years after the case of the impudent posture. It came in Boston, and it involved, appropriately, that prima ballerina of the law of obscenity, *Fanny Hill*. Two booksellers were convicted.[6] On their appeal, the upper court dismissed a number of points raised by the defense, but said absolutely nothing about whether the book was obscene. Apparently the answer was obvious.

Twenty years later, in its customary xenophobic

[5]It was a near thing though; twelve years after the first publication of the book, a dealer named Drybutter was put in the pillory for selling it.

[6]One of them was named Holmes, and considering the population of Boston in the early nineteenth century, we may speculate on the degree of consanguinity between the convict and the celebrated physician-literatteur and that great man of law, his son.

mood, Congress moved to guard against infection from abroad; in passing a tariff act, it authorized Customs officials to confiscate pictures. But this was rather limited, and we still had no definition of obscenity.

England sent us one. It came in the form of judicial interpretation of a statute. Parliament, in 1857, enacted the first major piece of anti-obscenity legislation, Lord Campbell's Act. When people get morally indignant, they are apt to pass laws against things that are already illegal. Lord Campbell's Act was an example.[7]

The Act had to do with procedures for stamping out the crime, not with saying what it was. Definition came eleven years later in the case of *Queen* v. *Hicklin*. The case involved an anti-Catholic pamphlet, more libelous than obscene, published by the Protestant Electoral Union. The Lord Chief Justice formulated a test of obscenity that had an enduring and baleful influence in both Great Britain and the United States. He said:

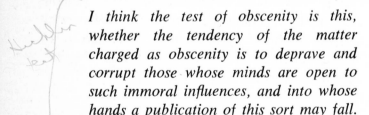

> *I think the test of obscenity is this, whether the tendency of the matter charged as obscenity is to deprave and corrupt those whose minds are open to such immoral influences, and into whose hands a publication of this sort may fall.*

[7]Another, more recent, was the Congressional tautology declaring it a crime to burn a draft card, when it was already a crime to be without one's draft card. Lord Campbell's Act at least affected the procedures for punishing obscene publication; the card-burning statute made no change in the penalties that already existed, which would apply whether one burned his card, threw it out the window, or chewed it up and swallowed it.

Meanwhile, things had been stirred up in the United States. Most of the stirring was done by Anthony Comstock. Remembered as an old bluenose, Comstock was in fact a young bluenose. In his early twenties he had made his reputation as a crusader against vice. In 1873, at the age of twenty-eight, he set a standard for all future lobbyists to shoot at: singlehanded, he got Congress to pass the archetype of American anti-obscenity legislation. There are very few Acts of Congress that bear the name of anyone other than a senator or representative: the mark of the man is that this statute is known as the Comstock Act. On the day of its passage, its author made a diary entry: "Oh how can I express the joy of my Soul or speak the mercy of God!" [8]

This rich vein of repressive legislation—sometimes referred to as the Comstock Load—provided the model for most American anti-obscenity statutes, and occupied the entire stage until a short time ago. In the past few years, Congressmen and state legislators, apprised of the existence of the First Amendment and deeply alarmed by it, have begun to fashion new statutes in an effort to overcome the recent decisions of the courts.

They had no problem with earlier decisions. Ameri-

---

[8]Comstock's famous organization, the New York Society for the Suppression of Vice, has not been heard from for a number of years. It appears as a complainant in the law reports until the 1930's (when it was under the direction of John Sumner) and then vanishes. Upon inquiry at the New York bureau that keeps records of the formation and dissolution of corporations, I found that the Society for the Suppression of Vice never died. It first changed its name, then merged, and now lives on, corporately, as the Police Athletic League.

can courts had eagerly adopted the *Hicklin* test, and used it to define obscenity in applying both the Comstock Act and the similar statutes that every state but one eventually enacted.[9]

In two respects the *Hicklin* rule was modified after a time. It had focused on "matter" rather than books. This permitted prosecutors to proceed against selected pages or paragraphs, and permitted courts to condemn a work though neither judge nor jury had read it through. By the end of the 1940's, however, many courts had held that a book should be judged as a whole, not on the basis of isolated pasages. The other change had to do with *Hicklin's* solicitude for the susceptible. It was gradually realized that what was published for the world at large should not be constricted by rules designed for minors; adult reading could not be reduced to the level of a child's bookshelf.

These modifications were sensible but peripheral. In its essence—"the tendency of the matter to deprave or corrupt"—*Hicklin* survived and flourished. Courts decided whether publication was permissible by deciding

[9]Both the federal statute and the typical state statute refer to material "obscene, lewd, lascivious" and, depending on the legislators' fancy, one or more additional near-synonyms. Congress, in a magnificent afterthought, enacted a statute in 1909 that added the word "filthy." The courts, however, have found it unnecessary to go beyond "obscene," treating the rest of the language as redundant or, at any rate, subsumed. The one state that did not follow the Congressional lead (though some of its municipalities have anti-obscenity ordinances) is New Mexico. In response to inquiry, New Mexico officials confirmed the void, but assured the inquirer that there was no greater incidence of sexual immorality in New Mexico than elsewhere.

whether a book was "lustful." If it was, it was obscene; and its author and publisher, criminals. As to how provocative a book must be to rate as lustful, the answer, of course, was subjective. Somewhat more charitable answers were given as time went on. But while the law of obscenity dropped a few gables and dormers as the memory of Campbell's queen and Comstock's congress began to fade, the underlying idea of *Hicklin* was not relinquished until a moment ago.

The famous *Ulysses* case, in 1934, made more of an impact upon commentators than upon the law. Apart from the support it gave to proponents of the whole-book rule, the decision actually confirmed the *Hicklin* test. Both the trial court and the appellate court were able to conclude that *Ulysses* was not really lustful. The "erotic passages," said the upper court, "are submerged in the book as a whole and have little resultant effect." And the district court had found that the sex in the book repelled rather than attracted. It was, in Judge Woolsey's words, "emetic, not aphrodisiac," the Judge thus elevating into legal principle the proposition that nausea is not immoral.

The censors were hardly checked. Shortly before the *Ulysses* case, a bookseller had been convicted of crime for selling Theodore Dreiser's *An American Tragedy*. The conviction was affirmed by one of America's most distinguished courts, the Supreme Judicial Court of Massachusetts. In the 1940's, Lillian Smith's *Strange Fruit* was held obscene; and still later so was Edmund

Wilson's *Memoirs of Hecate County*. Such decisions are
barely comprehensible to the present college generation,
yet they are scarcely older than those who find them so
astonishing.

Early in 1957, the Supreme Court struck down a
Michigan statute that defined obscenity as material having
a "deleterious influence upon youth." "Surely," said Justice Frankfurter, "this is to burn the house to roast the
pig." But the effect of the decision was simply to make
one of the *Hicklin* modifications, acknowledged in many
states, compulsory in all. A few months later, in the
famous *Roth* case, the Supreme Court held that state and
federal anti-obscenity laws that spoke in general terms
were valid. Affirming a pair of criminal convictions, the
Court sustained both the Comstock Law and one of its
statehouse nephews, an act of the California legislature.[10]
The second paring down of *Hicklin* was given sanction:
judgments could not rest on isolated passages. With these
familiar caveats, however, a solid majority ruled that
anti-obscenity statutes could stand against the First
Amendment guarantees.

The Court set out a definition of obscenity that in-

---

[10]What is popularly known as the *Roth* case is thus two cases, a matter
of some importance since Mr. Justice Harlan took the view that while the
First Amendment severely restricted federal attempts at suppression, state
governments should be allowed a wider leeway. Chief Justice Burger has
apparently joined Harlan in this view, and one of new Justice Blackmun's
first official actions indicates that he subscribes as well.

The defendant in the state case was named Alberts; it is not known
whether he was aggrieved by the fact that, for the accidental reason that
his case came second, he lost the title and has been denied the degree of
immortality achieved by Roth.

corporated the two limits upon *Hicklin,* suggested that frames of reference may change in time, and substituted the word "prurient" for "lustful." It added, among other things, that the decision merely confirmed the existing judicial view of the subject. One of the other things was to become important; but at the time it drew no attention.

The *Roth* decision was hailed as a victory for those bent on suppression. The majority opinion was widely accepted as one that gave constitutional approval to the established law of obscenity. There had been attacks on the *Comstock Act* and a typical state law, and the attacks had been repulsed. The favorite arguments of those who opposed censorship—that obscenity was impossible to define and that there was no demonstrable connection between exposure to it and anti-social behavior—had been explicitly rejected. There was some stately language about the importance of the First Amendment guarantees; but obscenity, the Court held, lay outside those guarantees.

Obscenity was given an elaborate definition, the prurient-interest formula, which the opinion said was only a summary of what most courts had already been saying. The two unpalatable elements of the *Hicklin* rule were no longer accepted. But otherwise the old law apparently remained intact. It might indeed be said that *Roth* had strengthened it. The intellectual minority was not going to have its way; the tastes of the avant-garde would not disrupt the restraints on publication that a majority morality required.

There was reason for the censors' satisfaction. Most students, including those who would have liked to see a change, agreed with this interpretation of the case. There are internal inconsistencies in the *Roth* opinion; one encounters items that simply do not fit. But on the face of it, the most plausible summary seems to be this:

> *The question is whether obscenity is protected by the First Amendment. It is not. This is demonstrated by the following:*
>
> *1. The Court has always assumed that obscenity is not protected.*
>
> *2. The First Amendment guarantees are not absolute; thirteen of the fourteen states that ratified the Constitution provided for the prosecution of criminal libel, and all fourteen made either blasphemy or profanity, or both, statutory crimes.*
>
> *3. Statutes and decisions, "sufficiently contemporaneous" with the ratification of the Constitution, indicate that obscenity was among the exceptions to the guarantees.*

There is a current misapprehension that the *Roth* opinion proclaimed the social value test. It did not, as Mr. Justice Clark pointed out with some vehemence in later cases. No one at the time suggested that it did. The first such suggestion came two years later in the *Lady Chatterley* case, and it came not from the bench but from counsel.

Roth did, however, contain the seed of the value test. An opinion is not itself a precedent. The precedent is the holding: the outcome of the litigation, together with the reasoning on which the outcome is based. The rest is *dictum*—persuasive perhaps, and influential, especially when the Supreme Court is speaking, but not binding upon future courts. The simple answer of *Roth* to the simple question raised is clear enough: anti-obscenity statutes are not, in general, forbidden by the First Amendment. But that cannot be the entire holding; the conclusion is not self-evident, and future courts might look to the reasons that supported it.

The reasons that the *Roth* majority stressed were not good. It was true that the Supreme Court "had always assumed that obscenity is not protected," but assumptions are not law; certain older courts had always assumed that heresy required burning. The judicial statements on which the majority relied came from opinions that had nothing to do with obscenity. They were offhand remarks, tossed off when obscenity was not in issue. *Dicta* so *obiter* cannot constitute precedent. The other reasons offered rest on constitutional history. But there is no specific evidence of the attitude toward obscenity of those who framed the First Amendment. The majority's historical argument is all inference, and the inference is unwarranted.

That the laws of the ratifying states provided punishment for libel, blasphemy, and profanity does not prove that the people were willing to give the federal government such power. Profanity in any event is a special case; a common use of it is the insult hurled in a charged social situation. It is close to action—the word "hurl" is indicative—something that may be restrained in the interest of peacekeeping. We cannot suppose that those who wrote the Bill of Rights would have agreed that a book should be censored because it contained profane statements. And the hypothesis becomes ludicrous when we consider blasphemy. The founding fathers were not seventeenth-century theocratic sectarians. They were eighteenth-century students of John Locke, divided on many points but united in a rational libertarian philosophy.[11]

It is certain that the Supreme Court, at the time when it decided *Roth,* would not have sanctioned the suppression of a book on the ground that it was profane or blasphemous. Yet if these colonial exceptions to freedom of speech were no longer tolerable, how did their terminated existence justify present-day punishment for obscenity? As for criminal libel, prosecutions have been so rare in our history that it may be questioned whether

[11]The Fourteenth Amendment, which came three-quarters of a century later, has been held to make the First Amendment, which speaks of Congress only, applicable to state governments as well. Thus the First Amendment must now be read as though it began "Neither Congress nor any state legislature shall make any law bridging. . . ." In searching history for the meaning of the guaranty, however, we must look to the restraints that the people of 1789 wished to put upon the new, mysterious and worrisome central government.

criminal libel is part of our law at all.

The history ends in anachronism. The majority opinion cites statutes and decisions as supplying "sufficiently contemporaneous evidence"—an odd concept—of the meaning of the First Amendment. None of them was, in fact, contemporaneous with the adoption of the Amendment. Their dates range from 1800 to 1843. But it would not matter if these statutes and decisions had more fitting dates. Even if something were part of the law in 1787, it does not follow that the framers of the Constitution meant to encapsulate that part. By its terms the Bill of Rights seeks to preserve certain features of Anglo-American law and to reject others, and to guard against certain practices governments had been known to engage in, whether or not pursuant to law. It is incongruous, even grotesque, to argue that whatever existed in colonial law was enshrined in a document that gave legal expression to a rebellion.

The assumption and the history, then, prove nothing. The First Amendment speaks of freedom; it does not speak of preserving patterns of sexual behavior. Some other reason must be found for the Court's conclusion.

Fasten onto the language of the Amendment: Congress shall make "no law abridging the freedom of speech and of the press." This is one of the plainer statements in the Bill of Rights; it is not like "due process of law" or "unreasonable search." The language appears to be unequivocal. So if there is something that seems to be speech or press and yet may be prohibited, the phenomenon must be accounted for. The Court's declared reasons do not account for it.

We can agree with the majority opinion that those who framed the First Amendment, when they used the words "freedom of speech or of the press," did not intend to embrace every utterance. There are recognized exclusions from the guaranty; obscenity, the *Roth* decision tells us, is one of them. But why is obscenity not protected? Let us consider the Court's statement about social importance. In form an adventitious aside, it could be something more. Parts of the opinion dressed as holding may be dicta; this ragged dictum may be holding. Obscenity can be thought of as utterance of so little value that it does not amount to "speech" or "press" within the meaning of the First Amendment. It can reasonably be said that the majesty of an organic charter of government was not intended to protect every insignificant mouthing, every worthless scrap of paper. The contrary can be said too, but the matter is at least arguable.

The interpretative summary that appeared a few pages back adheres as closely as possible to the language and structure of the opinion, but it is oversimplified in order to give consistency to a judicial statement that cannot count consistency among its virtues. If the opinion were, in fact, consistent and its reasoning strong, there would be no chance of getting a lower court to depart from its ostensible meaning. But here we have an opinion woven largely of dubious history and non sequiturs, and almost hidden among them, a thread of solid meaning. The precedent, one may argue, does not lie in the weaknesses of *Roth;* it lies in its strength.

If the Court's statement about social importance contains the true support of the decision, another step may be taken. Utter lack of social importance, it is said, justifies anti-obscenity laws. Then is that not a defining test of obscenity, so far as the Constitution is concerned? If there is speech that may be suppressed only because it has no value, then it is only speech wanting in value that may be suppressed. "The mark of suppressible obscenity," said counsel in the *Chatterley* case, "inheres in the constitutional justification of the suppressive legislation."

But in 1959 this was a lonely position. The initial comments in legal periodicals all agreed that the Court's prurient-interest formula was now the constitutional definition of obscenity, and made no suggestion that any other definition might exist. As time went on, and the views of important legal writers appeared, this was confirmed.[12]

There were two innovations in the defense of *Lady Chatterley.* One was the value theory—that if the work had literary merit, it was not utterly without social im-

[12]See, for example, Lockhart and McClure, 45 *Minnesota Law Review* 5 (1960); Paul and Schwartz, *Federal Censorship* (Glencoe, 1961); Gerber, 112 *University of Pennsylvania Law Review* 834 (1964). The only published indication of any agreement with the argument described came after the *Lady Chatterley* case had been decided: Kalven, "The Metaphysics of the Law of Obscenity" in *The Supreme Court Review* (University of Chicago Law School, 1960). As late as the fall of 1963, after the value theory had gained some acceptance in the courts, the American Book Publishers Council, always on the side of freedom, said that the theory did not apply where the work was "obscene and therefore beyond the pale of constitutional protection"—that is, the new argument that the work was not obscene applied only if the work was not obscene.

portance and hence it was protected by the First Amendment, no matter how it might fare under any other test of obscenity. The other, a corollary of the first, was a concession by defense counsel that readers might indeed buy and read the book for the sexual excitment it provided, that the book might fall into the theretofore fatal class called "lustful."

Literary witnesses had been used in earlier cases, but they were used in order to show that the literary qualities of the book were so overwhelming as to negate the sexual content; the reader's response, the witnesses sought to demonstrate, would be intellectual or aesthetic rather than lustful. Eminent critics and scholars (some of whom complained about the hypocrisy) were called upon to testify that the book in question was not really sexy or "pornographic" or "obscene." The approach in the *Chatterley* case was quite different. The defense presented two distinguished critics, Alfred Kazin and Malcolm Cowley, but they were brought to court to deal with the specific question of the literary merit of the book. If it was proven that the book had merit, counsel argued, then it could not be said to be "utterly without redeeming social importance."

The argument was refined and repeated in the welter of litigation that follow the publication of *Tropic of Cancer,* and a number of high state court judges accepted it. Indeed, the Supreme Judicial Court of Massachusetts, the court that convicted the bookseller Holmes in 1821 and had more recently held *An American Tragedy* and *Strange Fruit* to be obscene, was the first to give judicial sanction to the social value theory.[13] The conflict over *Tropic of Cancer* in the various state courts was settled, in favor of the book, by the Supreme Court in 1964, but the value theory gained acceptance from only two of the Justices, and one of them, Mr. Justice Goldberg, soon took another job.

If in the *Lady Chatterley* case counsel felt it disingenuous to employ the usual argument that the book was not really lustful, the point was all the plainer in *Fanny Hill.* The book does have some literary merit, but it is quite clear that its author meant to appeal to a direct, physiological interest in sex, and judging by the reactions of most readers, he succeeded. If provocation of sexual response—i.e., lustfulness—was still the test, the book must lose. It would win only if a majority of the Court held that there should be no suppression whatever for obscenity, or held that some degree of literary merit would give the book protection no matter how obscene it might be by traditional standards. There had to be five Justices who would subscribe to one or the other of these propositions.

There were. Black and Douglas adhered to their previously stated position that the First Amendment forbade all suppression for obscenity. Stewart had earlier held that only "hard-core pornography" might be suppressed, saying, without undertaking definition, that he knew it when he saw it. Now he made his test somewhat

---

[13]By a four-to-three decision. Later, again four-to-three, it ruled against *Fanny Hill*. Meanwhile, also by four-to-three dicisions, the highest court of New York ruled against *Tropic of Cancer* and in favor of *Fanny Hill.*

less of a Magic Automatic Self-Bailing Little Wonder; he accepted counsel's suggestion that the concept covered only materials that flunked all three criteria—the established (since 1957) prurient interest test, the pretty much established (since 1962) patent offensiveness test, and the knocking-at-the-door value theory. Harlan indicated his acceptance of the value theory where federal legislation was concerned, but voted against *Fanny Hill,* maintaining his position that the First Amendment had less effect on state action than on federal action.

The principal opinion was written by Brennan, and joined in by Warren and Fortas. For the Chief Justice, this represented a marked change in position; in earlier cases he had stated strongly that anti-book decisions by lower courts should rarely be upset. The opinion gave full and explicit expression to the value test:

> *. . . a book cannot be proscribed unless it is found to be* UTTERLY *without redeeming social value. This is so even though the book is found to possess the requisite prurient appeal and to be patently offensive. Each of the three federal constitutional criteria is to be applied independently; the social value of the book can neither be weighed against nor cancelled by its prurient appeal or patent offensiveness. . . .* (The emphasis is the Court's.)

White and Clark protested that *Roth* was never meant

to set up such a test, but the theory was now law. Four Justices gave it full approval, and a fifth recognized it as a proper construction of the First Amendment.[14] But whether three or four or five accepted the theory, the fact that two others would go even further constructed a solid precedent. As Judge Aldrich of the First Circuit suggested in a later case, if deuces are wild and you're holding three aces and two deuces, you've got five aces.

Two other obscenity cases were argued the same day, and decided the same day as *Fanny Hill.* In both, obscenity was found and convictions affirmed. One was *Ginzburg,* to which I have referred. The other was *Mishkin,* where the defendant's lawyers made no claim that the books in question had merit, and chose not to urge the social value test. These cases were lost, but by negative implication, they strengthened the precedent of *Fanny Hill.*

The courts below the level of the Supreme Court have regarded the precedent as established. So has the public. The concept of value as a legal determinant thus moved, in stages, from a casual dictum to an advocate's argument to a seriously-regarded legal theory and, finally, to a principle of law.[15]

---

[14]He would not apply the Amendment in its full vigor to state statutes.

[15]It then achieved the perhaps even more elevated status of common cliche. The phrase "redeeming social value" appeared regularly in newspapers and news broadcasts. One of its more interesting applications emerged in a conversation between a literary agent and an editor in a paperback publishing house. The book under discussion was primarily a sex-exploitaiton effort. The editor indicated a low opinion of its quality. The agent protested that no, really, the book had "some social value, some literary merit." The editor answered, "Don't worry. We can work around it."

That's where it is. Is it good? I think so, but first let me quote myself against myself. Three years ago I wrote:

> *The current uses of the new freedom are not all to the good. There is an acne on our culture. Books enter the best-seller lists distinguished only by the fact that once they would have put their publishers in jail. Advertising plays upon concupiscence in ways that range from foolish to fraudulent. Theater marquees promise surrogate thrills, and the movies themselves, even some of the good ones, include 'daring' scenes—'dare' is a child's word—that have no meaning except at the box office. Second-hand Freud gives the film director a line on which to hang his heroine's clothes; psycho-analytic cliches create his reputation as philosopher-poet, while shots of skin insure his solvency. Television commercials peddle sex with an idiot slyness. We approach a seductio ad absurdum. A visitor from outer space who had time to study only our art and entertainment would take back an eccentric view of the reproductive process on earth. This is indeed a lip-licking, damp-palmed age.*

I see no reason to amend, in 1970, this statement made in

1967. But I do not find it inconsistent with what is said above.

"Not all to the good" is different from "not good." And "acne" is appropriate. The symptoms constitute an unattractive aspect of our cultural adolescence; there are other aspects that are attractive. Moreover, acne is hardly fatal. After not too long a time, it generally goes away. What the quoted passage describes is, I think, a passing phase.

It is the middle-aged who are, in this regard, most adolescent. Younger people are less aroused by the new freedom of sexual expression, in both senses: not nearly so alarmed, and not nearly so titillated. The long refusal to permit honest treatment of sexual subjects, the long persistence of the mystical notion that certain words could not be uttered, have conditioned a nation of voyeurs. The customers at dirty book stores and at peep shows are not young.

Reactions to representations of sex, though they may be physiologically felt, are culturally conditioned. Pornography is in the groin of the beholder. The ugly phase will pass because it is not the freedom itself, but the taboo it displaces, that sets the stage for prurience.

Whether I was right or wrong in this prediction, the proposition that the end of literary censorship is good is not negated. This is because the constitutional issue overrides all else. The First Amendment does not exist to protect expression that is beneficial; it exists to protect expression. Indeed, if all it guarded was what we think is salutary, the Amendment would be surplusage. There is no need of a guaranty of freedom for what the majority wants. What is needed is a guaranty of freedom for what the majority does not want, or believes will do some harm, or believes will do great harm, or even hates with a quivering hate. The damage that may be done by expression deemed obscene is damage we must risk— must risk unless we are willing to abandon a fundamental principle of our political system. The question is not whether the uses of the new liberty are all to the good, or even whether they are good at all. The question is whether we are to have freedom of speech and press, with all the perils, jeopardy and fright that it entails.

*   *   *

I would agree that the words of the First Amendment cannot be taken literally and in their broadest sense. It is quite true, for example, that the Securities Act impairs the con man's freedom of speech. It is beyond the scope of this paper to say where all the lines are to be drawn, though I recommend the reader ponder such concepts as clear and present danger, direct and immediate injury, and expression brigaded with conduct. But wherever the lines be drawn, a book is pure expression. And to suppress a book in the interest of the prevailing sexual morality is, when we come to think of it, an odd thing, a very odd thing, indeed.

For there are moral values other than the sexual. Yet literary censorship has shown no interest in these other aspects of morality. No book has ever been suppressed on the ground that it promoted selfishness or dishonesty or cowardice. There have been some small efforts to restrict the portrayal of violence; the chief effect has been to tone down comic books, and to remit impressionable young minds to television and the newspapers for their daily ration of sadism. With this minuscule exception—and even here the target that attracts the most attention is sexual violence rather than violence itself—sex, together with heresy and sedition, has been the censors' preoccupation.

The outrageously immoral fact is that the only morality for whose sake the law has been willing to suppress books is sexual morality. Even if the attempt held a promise of success—even if it were true—and to my mind it is not—that worthy sexual behavior is retarded rather than advanced by freedom of expression, we would be denying freedom of speech and press in order to deal with just one small corner of morality. Proponents of sexual censorship must take the position that conformity to sexual convention is more important than honesty, than kindness, than courage. That position is, I think, not rational or decent.

*   *   *

We often hear freedom recommended on the theory that if all expression is permitted, the truth is bound to win. I disagree. In the short term, falsehood seems to do about as well. Even for longer periods, there can be no assurance of truth's victory; but over the long term, the likelihood is high. And certainly truth's chances are better with freedom than with repression.

"The best test of truth," said Justice Holmes, "is the power of the thought to get itself accepted in the competition of the market." [19] It is on this and other grounds related to the working of our political system that we most often hear the First Amendment justified: freedom of expression is necessary to make democracy work.

The usual arguments, however, are made from society's point of view; they are political arguments. There is another reason for freedom of expression. It does not have to do with our society or our government; it concentrates rather on the individual.

Among the things that make life valuable is the kind of internal activity that can roughly be called thought. This includes both thought in the strict sense, whose more elegant products are philosophy and science, and thought in its emotive aspects, whose more elegant product is art. But thought is frustrated and tends to rot if it must be contained within the individual. In *Areopagitica,* Milton's general arguments became at one point intensely personal: "Give me liberty to know, to utter, and to argue freely according to conscience, above all liberties."

Aside from the collective gain that comes from the free interchange of ideas, there is a direct personal value for the individual concerned. Each of us should have the

---

[19]The figure of speech, an interesting conjunction of capitalism and intellectual freedom, had earlier been used by Jefferson. I would transpose and amend it slightly: It is in open exchange that truth has the best chance to get itself accepted.

right to speak his thoughts and to hear the thoughts of others. The warrant needs no words like "high" or "noble." The freedom simply makes us feel good.

The First Amendment grants this political benefit and this personal benefit; and if their enjoyment brings with it, as frequently it does, the disagreeable, the offensive, even that which is dangerous to established morals— why, these are no more than the necessary sequels of a very great good grant.

Perhaps best known for his books, lectures, and articles concerning jazz—both the music and the performers—Nat Hentoff has been a staff writer for THE NEW YORKER *since 1960. His articles have also appeared in* EVERGREEN REVIEW, COMMONWEAL, PLAYBOY, THE NEW YORK TIMES, *and in the* NEW REPUBLIC.

Mr. Hentoff received his B.A. from Northeastern University and did his post-graduate studies at Harvard. He was selected as a Fulbright fellow to the Sorbonne in Paris.

For several years, Mr. Hentoff was the writer, producer, and announcer in radio. In turn, he was associate editor for DOWN BEAT *magazine and co-founder and co-editor of* THE JAZZ REVIEW.

Author of many books, Nat Hentoff is best known for OUR CHILDREN ARE DYING, JOURNEY INTO JAZZ, *and* A POLITICAL LIFE: THE EDUCATION OF JOHN V. LINDSAY.

Nat Hentoff

The censor is always quick to justify his functions in terms that are protective of society. But the First Amendment, written in terms that are absolute, deprives the State of any power to pass on the value, the propriety, or the morality of a particular expression.

> Justice William O. Douglas,
> MEMOIRS *v.* MASSACHUSETTS,
> *383 U.S. 413* (*The* FANNY HILL
> *case, 1966*)

IN ONE SENSE, I FIND IT REMARKABLE—as well as dismaying—that censorship is still a subject for debate. The Constitution could not be more clear: "Congress shall make no law abridging the freedom of speech, or of the press," says the First Amendment. And that means, as Justices Douglas and Black have consistently maintained, freedom of expression in any form. ("I read *no law abridging,*" Justice Black added in the 1957 Roth case, "to mean NO LAW ABRIDGING.")

However, considering all the other attempts to blunt the Bill of Rights—from secret surveillance to the eerie notion of preventive detention—it is not remarkable, after all, that the fundamental right of freedom of expression is still under siege in a country where many, including members of the judiciary, continue to feel that wholly free expression will somehow endanger the republic.

It is rather poignant, for example, to see Supreme Court Justice Potter Stewart stubbornly insist that what he calls "hard-core pornography" must be prohibited, although he is utterly unable to define what he means by the term. "I may not be able to come up with a definition of pornography," he has unhappily conceded, "but I certainly know it when I see it." A frail foundation, to say the least, for a decision by a Supreme Court Justice, but it is indicative of the fear that possesses otherwise rational men—the fear that freedom of expression can go "too far." Especially when sex is at issue.

We are making some progress, admittedly, in combating those fears—at least in the Court. In 1969, Justice Thurgood Marshall, writing the majority opinion in *Stanley* v. *Georgia* (394 U.S. 557), finally prohibits "making mere private possession of obscene material a crime." The once beleaguered Mr. Stanley had been found to have three reels of "obscene" film in his home. Justice Marshall concluded:

> *If the First Amendment means anything, it means that a State has no business telling a man, sitting alone in his own house, what books he may read or what films he may watch. Our whole constitutional heritage rebels at the thought of giving government the power to control men's minds.*

But if government does not have the power to control what a man may read or see at home, why should it have any power to control what he *voluntarily* chooses to read or see *outside* his home—in a bookstore, in a movie house, in a 25-cent "peep show" at Times Square, in a theatre?

Part of the traditional answer is that the citizenry must be protected from exposure to obscenity. Justice Marshall, in the Stanley case, held to the concept that there is such a phenomenon as obscenity. Mr. Stanley's films, the decision held, *were* obscene, but so long as he kept them home, he was not contaminating anybody else.

So we are now left to do battle with those who would prohibit obscenity in places to which the public has access. But what *is* obscenity? Or pornography? According to the Roth decision, the criterion for the determination of obscenity is "whether to the average person, applying contemporary community standards, the dominant theme of the material taken as a whole appeals to the prurient interest." Obscenity is also defined, the Court underlined in the *Fanny Hill* case, as being "utterly without social value."

What, then, are we to make of the Hassidic rabbi from Williamsburgh, who likes to look at the magazines in the Times Square stores specializing in erotica? "There's nothing as beautiful as God's creations," is the way he explains his avocation. (*New York Post,* June 2, 1970). If he finds evidence of God in, let us say, the *New York Review of Sex,* by what right, in law, can anyone mandate that what he's looking at is "utterly without social value"?

To *whom?*

Consider, moreover, the absurdity of making the arousal of "prurient interest" in *any way* a test of the legality of a book, a magazine, a film, a play. As Lionel Trilling wrote in a review of *Lolita:*

> *Since it's a legitimate function of art to arouse feelings of love of country or of God or of family, why shouldn't it be a legitimate function of art to arouse thoughts of lust?*

And on what possible Constitutional grounds can one justify the application of "contemporary community standards" (granted, for argument's sake, that these can be really determined) to any *individual's* right of expression—or his right to enjoy the results of someone else's expression—so long as no one is *forced* to buy a book or see a movie or see a play?

Ah, but an individual can be so aroused by obscenity, by pornography—impossible as these are for even Justice Stewart to define—that he will do harm to others. But where's the proof? The overwhelming evidence is that there is no such proof. Certainly, few have looked more zealously for such proof than the Reverend Morton A. Hill, president of *Morality in Media* and a member of the Presidential Commission on Obscenity and Pornography.

With great sadness, he has concluded (*New York Sunday News,* May 31, 1970) that:

> *It is impossible to prove that an individual obscene item is the effective cause of a specific crime. The whole person is the cause of an act, not a particular item. I'm afraid the commission I'm on will conclude that it can't be proven that the smut industry has any bad effect on people.*

To which Dr. Ann Ruth Terkel, a psychiatrist and faculty member of the William Alanson White Institute, adds:

> *There is no clinical evidence to support statements that pornography can even affect already disturbed youngsters in a detrimental manner.*

But let us pursue this theme further to see how completely impossible it is to know how to "protect" society by censorship. In his concurring opinion in *Memoirs* v. *Massachusetts,* Justice Douglas, in the main body of his text, cites an article (Murphy, "The Value of Pornography") in a 1964 issue of the *Wayne Law Review.* Then, in a footnote, the Justice, to indicate how futile it would be "even for a censor to remove all that might possibly stimulate sexual conduct," quotes from Murphy:

The majority (of individuals), needless to say, are somewhere in between the over-scrupulous extremes of excitement and frigidity . . . Within this variety, it is impossible to define 'hard-core' pornography, as if there were some singly lewd concept from which all profane ideas passed by imperceptible degrees into that sexuality called holy. But there is no 'hard core.' Everything, every idea, is capable of being obscene if the personality perceiving it so apprehends it.

It is for this reason that books, pictures, charades, ritual, the spoken word can and do lead to conduct harmful to the self indulging in it and to others. Heinrich Pommerenke, who was a rapist, abuser, and mass slayer of women in Germany, was prompted in his series of ghastly deeds by Cecil B. DeMille's "The Ten Commandments." During the scene of the Jewish women dancing about the Golden Calf, all the doubts of his life came clear: Women were the source of the world's trouble and it was his mission to punish them for this and to execute them. Leaving the theatre, he slew his first victim in a park nearby.

John George Haigh, the British vampire who sucked his victims' blood through

> *soda straws and dissolved their drained*
> *bodies in acid baths, first had his murder-*
> *inciting dreams and vampire-longings*
> *from watching the 'voluptuous' procedure*
> *of—an Anglican High Church Service!*

But even if one grants Murphy's argument, the young —surely the young—must be protected against obscenity and pornography. In Denmark where pornography in all forms is more legally accessible than in any other Western country, there are age restrictions; but I doubt if these restrictions cannot be insurmounted by diligent youngsters. In any case, the Danish Medical-Legal Council has concluded that a child's psycho-sexual development is determined primarily by his family and his peers:

> *It is inconceivable that coarse external*
> *influences such as pornography should be*
> *of any significance in the sexual develop-*
> *ment of children and adolescents.*

Concurring, Hans Hessellund, a researcher at the Psychological Laboratory at the University of Copenhagen, emphasizes:

> *What's bad for young people is their*
> *parents' attitude toward sex—their feel-*
> *ings that sex is dirty.*

Furthermore, as Richard Schickel, writing of film

censorship, points out (*The Progressive,* September, 1969):

> *It is impossible to place on the screen any sexual fantasy wilder than that which is going on, at various times, in the mind of an eager adolescent. It is impossible, too, to portray as much violence up there on the screen as he dreams of wreaking on his adult oppressors, or to be more scornfully satirical of conventional wisdom than he is, or more questioning of received values. So how can anything he sees on the screen stimulate him more than consultation with himself or with his buddies at the candy store?*

In sum, Justice Douglas is exactly right. Any form of censorship violates the First Amendment, and in addition, cannot protect society. On the other hand, laws permitting censorship do have deleterious effects. As a Subcommittee Report on American Civil Liberties Union Policy Concerning Obscenity and Censorship makes clear:

> *The very possibility that (an obscenity) statute may be invoked provides a potent tool for suppression even of works that clearly are not obscene by the Court's definition . . . A bookseller or motion pic-*

> *ture exhibitor cannot afford to fight his
> way to the Supreme Court to determine
> whether a book or a picture has 'redeem-
> ing social importance' or does not appeal
> to 'prurient interest.' So long as the Courts
> deny him full First Amendment protec-
> tion, he will remain vulnerable to . . .
> grass-roots censorship. Under pressure, he
> will not sell a book or exhibit a motion
> picture which local officials claim is ob-
> scene.*

Censorship in any form is not only unnecessary—and I agree with Justices Douglas and Black, unconstitutional —but it is, and it has been, and it always will be, so long as any of it lasts, demonstrably harmful. Along with inhibiting free expression and free choice by the reader or viewer, censorship helps sustain the dangerous illusion that morality can be legislated and thereby improved.

The Reverend John R. Graham, First Universalist Church of Denver, gets to the core of this debate that should have ended long ago:

> *Until we learn to respect ourselves enough
> that we leave each other alone, we cannot
> discover the meaning of morality.*

Index

Index